Unwavering Focus: Journey to Excellence through Philippians 3:12-14

DERICK CHIBILU and Unwavering Focus

Published by Books By Derick Chibilu, 2024.

Table of Contents

"Unwavering Focus"

Journey to Excellence through Philippians 3:12-14

BY

DERICK CHIBILU

****

A Motivational Masterpiece

Published by Books by Derick Chibilu

12000 Sawmill Rd , The Woodlands,

TX, United States, Texas

Website: www.booksbyderikchibilu.com

Contact Number: +1 346-328-1110

Publication Date: 04/10/2024

Cover design by Dacisco Video and Media Production Team

Publisher's Note:

"Welcome to Unwavering Focus: Journey to Excellence through Philippians 3:12-" This book isn't just a read; it's a life-changing experience. Dive into "Unwavering Focus" and embark on a journey that will elevate your aspirations, empower your actions, and redefine your path to excellence.

For permission requests, please contact the publisher at the address provided above or you can visit our www.booksbyderickchibilu.com.[1]

Description

Embark on a life-transforming journey with "Unwavering Focus: Journey to Excellence through Philippians 3:12-14," a motivational masterpiece inspired by a powerful message preached by Pastor Larry Emmerson of North Central Assemblies of God Church of Spring Texas, USA, on Sunday, January 28, 2024, *titled "Focus, Forget, and Moving Forward" from Philippians 3:12 - 14.* This empowering guide navigates the principles of focus, forgetting the past, and moving forward to achieve unparalleled success in every aspect of life.

"Unwavering Focus" isn't just a book; it's a transformative guide that will reshape your mindset, empower your actions, and propel you toward unparalleled success. In this masterfully crafted work, we delve deep into the profound teachings of Philippians 3:12-14, unlocking a wealth of wisdom that transcends the boundaries of personal and professional growth.

As you embark on this inspirational journey, you can expect:

Profound Insights: Immerse yourself in the timeless teachings of Philippians, gaining profound insights into the principles of focus, forgetting the past, and moving forward. Each chapter is a revelation, offering practical applications for your everyday life.

Practical Wisdom: This book isn't just about theory; it's a practical guide to implementing Philippians principles in various aspects of life. From career advancement to personal relationships, you'll find actionable steps to cultivate a focused and purpose-driven existence.

Motivational Narratives: Through real-life examples and motivational narratives, you'll witness the transformative power of applying Philippians wisdom. Learn from the experiences of others who have embraced these principles and achieved remarkable success.

Holistic Approach: "Unwavering Focus" takes a holistic approach to personal development. It explores the synergy between focus, faith, relationships, health, and wealth, providing a comprehensive roadmap to living a fulfilled and balanced life.

Relevance to Diverse Audiences: Whether you're an aspiring professional, a sports enthusiast, a devoted family person, or a global citizen, this book caters to diverse audiences. Each chapter is tailored to resonate with different facets of life, ensuring that every reader finds valuable takeaways.

Expertly Curated Chapters: The 30 motivational chapters cover a wide array of topics, including sports, career, relationships, health, and more. Each chapter is expertly curated to make this book an indispensable resource for personal growth and achievement.

Why should you read "Unwavering Focus"?

Achieve Unprecedented Success: Discover the secrets to achieving unparalleled success by adopting a mindset rooted in focus, resilience, and forward momentum.

Overcome Challenges: Learn how to overcome challenges and setbacks with grace, using the timeless principles outlined in Philippians 3:12-14 as your guide.

Personal Transformation: Experience a profound personal transformation as you implement the practical advice and motivational insights shared throughout the book.

Inspiration for All Areas of Life: Whether you seek success in your career, relationships, health, or personal pursuits, "Unwavering Focus" offers inspiration and guidance for every area of your life.

This book isn't just a read; it's a life-changing experience. Dive into "Unwavering Focus" and embark on a journey that will elevate your aspirations, empower your actions, and redefine your path to excellence.

Chapter One: Introduction - Embracing the Philippians Mindset

Welcome to the transformative journey of "Unwavering Focus: Journey to Excellence through Philippians 3:12-14." In this introductory chapter, we embark on a quest to explore the profound teachings encapsulated in the verses of Philippians, unlocking a mindset that will redefine the way you approach challenges, success, and personal growth.

The Essence of Philippians 3:12-14

The verses from Philippians 3:12-14 lay the foundation for our expedition into a mindset of unparalleled focus, resilience, and forward momentum. The Apostle Paul's words resonate with timeless wisdom, inviting us to embrace a mindset that acknowledges past experiences while fervently pursuing a future filled with purpose and achievement.

"Not that I have already obtained this or am already perfect, but I press on to make it my own because Christ Jesus has made me his own. Brothers, I do not consider that I have made it my own. But one thing I do: forgetting what lies behind and straining forward to what lies ahead, I press on toward the goal for the prize of the upward call of God in Christ Jesus." - Philippians 3:12-14 (ESV)

Unveiling the Philippians Mindset

1. Acknowledging Imperfection:

Embrace the humility of acknowledging that perfection is a journey, not a destination. Understand that continuous improvement is a testament to our commitment to growth.

2. Pressing on with Purpose:

Just as Paul pressed on toward his goal, we too are challenged to define and pursue our aspirations with unwavering dedication. Find your purpose, and let it be the driving force behind your every endeavor.

3. Letting Go of the Past:

The art of forgetting is a powerful tool for personal transformation. Explore the liberating concept of leaving behind past failures, regrets, and doubts, creating space for new opportunities and triumphs.

4. Straining Forward to the Future:

A forward-focused mindset propels us towards greatness. Learn how to set ambitious yet achievable goals, creating a roadmap for success in all areas of life.

5. The Prize of the Upward Call:

Discover the ultimate reward – not just material success, but a higher calling that transcends worldly achievements. Uncover the spiritual and personal fulfillment that comes with aligning your goals with a purpose greater than yourself.

Setting the Stage for Your Journey

As we delve into each chapter, we will apply the Philippians mindset to various facets of life, offering practical guidance and actionable steps to bring about transformation. Whether you are seeking success in your career, striving for excellence in relationships, or pursuing personal growth, the principles outlined in Philippians 3:12-14 will serve as your guiding light.

Get ready to unlock the full potential of your life as we explore the transformative power of unwavering focus. Your journey toward excellence begins now, and "Unwavering Focus" is your compass.

Embracing Continuous Learning

In our pursuit of the Philippians mindset, we acknowledge that the journey toward excellence is a continuous learning experience. Each chapter in this book serves as a steppingstone, offering insights and practical applications that align with the timeless wisdom of Philippians 3:12-14. As we explore diverse aspects of life, we invite you to engage actively, absorb the teachings, and apply them to your unique circumstances.

A Blueprint for Success

Consider this book as your blueprint for success, meticulously crafted to guide you through the challenges and triumphs of life. The Philippians mindset becomes more than just a philosophy; it transforms into a strategic approach to navigating the complexities of the modern world. Whether you are an IT professional, a sports enthusiast, a devoted Christian, or someone passionate about continuous learning, "Unwavering Focus" is tailored to resonate with your aspirations.

Practical Applications in Every Chapter

Each chapter is designed not only to inspire but to empower. From the boardroom to the soccer field, from personal relationships to financial mastery, you will find practical applications that resonate with your daily life. We integrate the essence of Philippians 3:12-14 into tangible strategies, ensuring that these ancient teachings remain relevant and actionable in our contemporary context.

The Unique Blend of Spirituality and Practicality

"Unwavering Focus" stands out as a beacon of inspiration by seamlessly blending spirituality with practicality. This unique approach sets the stage for a holistic transformation, guiding you toward a life of purpose, achievement, and fulfillment. As you embark on this journey, you will witness the convergence of ancient wisdom with modern application, creating a powerful synergy that propels you toward your goals.

Your Invitation to Greatness

This book is not just a read; it's an invitation to greatness. The Philippians mindset is not a one-size-fits-all solution but a versatile tool that you can tailor to your aspirations and circumstances. Each chapter is an opportunity to unlock new dimensions of your potential, fostering a sense of purpose that extends beyond the pages and into the fabric of your everyday life.

As you turn the pages of "Unwavering Focus," remember that this isn't just a book; it's a companion on your journey toward excellence. Embrace the Philippians mindset, apply the lessons with intentionality, and watch as your life transforms into a masterpiece of focus, resilience, and forward momentum.

Your unparalleled journey begins now.

Chapter Two: The Power of Unyielding Focus

In the heart of your journey toward excellence lies the transformative force of unyielding focus. Building upon the foundation laid by Philippians 3:12-14, this chapter explores the profound impact of directing your energy, attention, and determination towards a singular purpose. Brace yourself for an exploration into the depths of human potential and the extraordinary achievements that become possible when focus becomes your guiding light.

The Core of Philippians Wisdom

"But one thing I do: forgetting what lies behind and straining forward to what lies ahead, I press on toward the goal for the prize of the upward call of God in Christ Jesus." - Philippians 3:13-14 (ESV)

These verses encapsulate the essence of unyielding focus. Forget the distractions of the past, strain forward to the future, and press on toward your goals with determination. In this chapter, we dissect each element, unveiling the power within the Philippians mindset.

1. Forgetting What Lies Behind

The Liberating Act of Letting Go

Explore the liberating concept of leaving behind past mistakes, failures, and missed opportunities. Learn how the act of forgetting empowers you to create a clean slate, allowing room for growth, innovation, and the pursuit of new achievements. Uncover the secrets of resilience and how the ability to let go contributes to unyielding focus.

2. Straining Forward to What Lies Ahead

The Forward Momentum of Purpose

Discover the forward momentum generated by a clear sense of purpose. We delve into the significance of setting ambitious yet attainable goals, creating a roadmap that propels you toward your aspirations. Understand how a future-focused mindset acts as a catalyst for personal and professional success.

3. Pressing on Toward the Goal

The Pursuit of Excellence

Embark on the journey of pressing on toward your goals with unwavering determination. Explore practical strategies to overcome obstacles, stay motivated, and maintain momentum in the face of challenges. This section serves as your guide to cultivating resilience and perseverance in the pursuit of excellence.

4. The Prize of the Upward Call

Beyond Material Success

What is the ultimate prize of the upward call? This section transcends traditional notions of success, inviting you to explore a higher purpose that aligns with your values and beliefs. Understand how the Philippians mindset leads not only to worldly achievements but also to a sense of fulfillment that goes beyond material success.

Building Your Unyielding Focus Toolkit

In the concluding sections of this chapter, we provide practical tools and exercises to help you cultivate unyielding focus in your daily life. From mindfulness practices to goal-setting techniques, you'll find actionable steps to strengthen your ability to stay focused, driven, and purposeful.

As you navigate the pages of "The Power of Unyielding Focus," remember that focus isn't just about narrowing your vision; it's about amplifying the intensity of your efforts toward what truly matters. This chapter lays the groundwork for the rest of your journey, setting the stage for a life characterized by purpose, determination, and unparalleled success.

Unleash the power of unyielding focus and watch as your goals transform from aspirations into tangible achievements.

Embracing Concentrated Energy

In the world of unyielding focus, your energy becomes a potent force. This chapter explores how concentrating your energy on specific goals magnifies your impact. As you immerse yourself in the teachings of Philippians 3:12-14, understand that your energy is a precious resource, and directing it purposefully leads to extraordinary outcomes.

1. The Magnifying Glass of Concentration

Explore the analogy of concentration as a magnifying glass, focusing the scattered rays of your energy into a powerful, concentrated beam. Learn how this concentrated energy enhances your effectiveness in every pursuit, from professional endeavors to personal growth.

2. Eliminating Distractions

Delve into practical strategies for eliminating distractions in an age of constant information bombardment. Discover how a clutter-free mind becomes a fertile ground for cultivating unyielding focus, enabling you to navigate challenges with clarity and precision.

3. The Alchemy of Single-Minded Pursuit

Uncover the alchemy that occurs when you commit to a single-minded pursuit. We dissect the power of sustained focus on a singular goal, revealing how it transforms challenges into steppingstones and aspirations into tangible achievements.

**The Ripple Effect of Unyielding Focus

The impact of unyielding focus extends beyond personal achievements; it creates a ripple effect that influences those around you. This section explores how your focused efforts can inspire and elevate others, creating a culture of excellence and determination in your professional and personal spheres.

1. Leadership through Focused Vision

For leaders and aspiring leaders, discover how a focused vision can galvanize teams, fostering a sense of purpose and unity. Learn the art of leading by example, inspiring others to embrace the Philippians mindset of unyielding focus.

2. Nurturing Relationships with Intentionality

Explore the role of focus in nurturing meaningful relationships. Learn how being present in each interaction, whether personal or professional, contributes to the strength and depth of connections. Discover the importance of intentional focus in fostering empathy, understanding, and trust.

**Your Unyielding Focus Toolkit: Strategies for Daily Practice

As you conclude this chapter, find practical exercises and tools to integrate unyielding focus into your daily routine. From time management techniques to mindfulness practices, these tools will become your allies in cultivating and sustaining the power of unyielding focus.

Unleash Your Unyielding Focus

Chapter Two serves as a cornerstone for the subsequent chapters, laying the groundwork for a life characterized by purpose, determination, and unparalleled success. As you embrace the teachings of Philippians 3:12-14, remember that your journey toward excellence is fueled by the unwavering power of unyielding focus.

Unleash this power, and witness your goals transform from distant aspirations into tangible, extraordinary achievements.

Chapter Three: Forgetting Failures, Embracing Growth

In the canvas of your journey towards excellence, the strokes of growth are painted over the canvas of failures. This chapter, inspired by the wisdom of Philippians 3:12-14, unravels the transformative power of forgetting past failures and wholeheartedly embracing the process of growth. Prepare to explore how the ability to learn from setbacks becomes a catalyst for personal and professional advancement.

The Canvas of Growth Amidst Failures

"But one thing I do: forgetting what lies behind and straining forward to what lies ahead, I press on toward the goal for the prize of the upward call of God in Christ Jesus." - Philippians 3:13-14 (ESV)

Philippians lay the groundwork for this chapter, emphasizing the importance of not being burdened by past failures. Instead, view them as steppingstones towards personal growth, resilience, and ultimate success.

1. Lessons from Failure: A Roadmap to Success

Turning Setbacks into Steppingstones

Explore how failures are not roadblocks but opportunities for growth. Learn to extract valuable lessons from each setback, transforming them into steppingstones towards your goals. Understand that every failure brings you closer to success if approached with the right mindset.

2. Embracing a Growth Mindset

Cultivating a Mindset of Possibilities

Delve into the concept of a growth mindset – a belief that intelligence and abilities can be developed through dedication and hard work. Uncover strategies to shift from a fixed mindset, where failure is seen as a reflection of one's abilities, to a growth mindset, where failures are viewed as opportunities to learn and improve.

3. Resilience in the Face of Adversity

Building Inner Strength

Examine the role of resilience in overcoming adversity. Understand how a resilient mindset enables you to bounce back stronger after failures, fostering the ability to adapt, grow, and thrive amidst challenges.

4. From Setbacks to Comebacks: Real-Life Stories

Inspiring Narratives of Triumph Over Failure

Embark on a journey through real-life stories of individuals who turned their failures into triumphs. Discover how embracing growth transformed setbacks into comebacks and learn from the resilience and determination that characterize their inspiring narratives.

Embracing Growth in Various Aspects of Life

The chapter concludes by applying the principles of forgetting failures and embracing growth to diverse areas of life, including career, relationships, health, and personal development.

1. Career Advancement through Growth

Explore strategies for leveraging professional setbacks as opportunities for skill development and career advancement. Learn how a growth mindset accelerates your climb up the corporate ladder.

2. Strengthening Relationships through Personal Growth

Understand how personal growth enhances your ability to build meaningful connections. Explore the dynamics of relationships and how the lessons learned from failures contribute to stronger, more authentic bonds.

3. Health and Wellness: A Journey of Continuous Improvement

Discover the role of growth in the realm of health and wellness. Uncover practices that promote physical and mental well-being, emphasizing the importance of embracing growth in your journey towards a healthier lifestyle.

Your Growth Toolkit: Practical Strategies for Daily Application

As you conclude this chapter, find practical tools and exercises to implement the principles of forgetting failures and embracing growth in your daily life. These tools will become your allies in cultivating a mindset that transforms setbacks into opportunities for continuous improvement.

The Transformative Power of Embracing Growth

Chapter Three lays the foundation for the chapters that follow, setting the stage for a life characterized by resilience, adaptability, and an unwavering commitment to growth. As you embrace the teachings of Philippians 3:12-14, remember that your journey towards excellence is not defined by failures but by the growth that arises from them.

Embrace growth and watch as failures become mere steppingstones on your path to extraordinary success.

Unveiling the Potential Within Failure

In the intricate tapestry of life, failures are not the threads of defeat but the fibers that weave the fabric of success. This chapter unveils the potential within failure, drawing inspiration from the wisdom of Philippians 3:12-14. Explore how each stumble, setback, or disappointment becomes a canvas for growth, providing an opportunity to redefine your narrative.

1. Reconstructing Failure as Feedback

Shift your perspective on failure, viewing it not as a definitive endpoint but as feedback. Learn how to extract valuable insights from every misstep, guiding your journey towards continuous improvement and mastery.

2. Embracing Vulnerability as a Source of Strength

Discover the strength that arises from embracing vulnerability. Understand that acknowledging failure is not a sign of weakness but a courageous step towards growth. Explore how vulnerability becomes the bridge to resilience and self-discovery.

The Growth Mindset: A Beacon of Possibilities

The journey from failure to growth is illuminated by the beacon of a growth mindset. Delve deeper into the intricacies of this mindset, understanding its transformative power in navigating challenges and seizing opportunities for advancement.

1. Navigating the Peaks and Valleys with Equanimity

Learn to navigate the peaks and valleys of life with equanimity. A growth mindset fosters resilience, enabling you to approach challenges with a calm and focused demeanor, knowing that each experience contributes to your evolution.

2. The Growth Feedback Loop: Iterate, Adapt, Thrive

Uncover the essence of the growth feedback loop – a continuous cycle of iteration, adaptation, and thriving. Explore how this loop propels you forward, transforming setbacks into steppingstones and failures into triumphs.

Real-Life Narratives: Turning Failures into Triumphs

Immerse yourself in inspiring narratives of individuals who transformed their darkest moments into sources of strength. From business magnates to athletes, witness how the resilience born from failure became the driving force behind their extraordinary achievements.

1. Entrepreneurial Resilience: Lessons from Setbacks

Explore the entrepreneurial landscape, discovering how setbacks and failures are integral to the journey of building successful enterprises. Learn from real-life stories of entrepreneurs who turned challenges into opportunities for innovation and growth.

2. Sporting Triumphs: The Resilience of Athletes

Enter the arena of sports and witness how athletes, guided by the principles of Philippians 3:12-14, turned defeats into comebacks. Their stories exemplify the indomitable spirit cultivated through embracing growth in the face of adversity.

Applying Growth Principles Across Domains

The chapter concludes by applying the principles of forgetting failures and embracing growth to various domains, offering actionable insights for personal and professional development.

1. Career Mastery through Growth Mindset

Unlock strategies for leveraging failures as steppingstones in your professional journey. Embrace a growth mindset that positions setbacks as opportunities for skill enhancement and career advancement.

2. Nurturing Resilient Relationships

Understand the role of growth in building resilient relationships. Learn how the lessons gleaned from failures contribute to more authentic connections and deeper bonds.

3. Wellness and Growth: A Holistic Approach

Embark on a holistic journey of wellness and growth. Discover practices that promote physical and mental well-being, emphasizing the importance of embracing growth in your pursuit of a healthier lifestyle.

Your Growth Toolkit: Practical Strategies for Daily Application

As you conclude this chapter, find practical tools and exercises to integrate the principles of forgetting failures and embracing growth into your daily life. These tools will serve as your companions in cultivating a mindset that transforms setbacks into steppingstones on your path to excellence.

The Triumph of Growth Over Failure

Chapter Three lays the foundation for the chapters to come, setting the stage for a life characterized by resilience, adaptability, and an unwavering commitment to growth. As you embrace the teachings of Philippians 3:12-14, remember that your journey towards excellence is not marred by failures but embellished by the growth that emerges from them.

Embrace growth and witness the triumph of resilience and determination over the challenges that pave your way to extraordinary success.

Chapter Four: Moving Forward with Purpose

———

In the tapestry of our journey towards excellence, the threads of purpose weave a narrative that transcends the ordinary. Inspired by the profound guidance of Philippians 3:12-14, this chapter unfolds the significance of moving forward with purpose – a beacon that illuminates the path to personal and professional fulfillment. Prepare to embark on a journey where every step is infused with intentionality, guided by a sense of purpose that propels you towards your aspirations.

Philippians 3:12-14 as the Guiding Light

"Not that I have already obtained this or am already perfect, but I press on to make it my own because Christ Jesus has made me his own. Brothers, I do not consider that I have made it my own. But one thing I do: forgetting what lies behind and straining forward to what lies ahead, I press on toward the goal for the prize of the upward call of God in Christ Jesus." - Philippians 3:12-14 (ESV)

These verses form the compass that directs our journey in this chapter, emphasizing the active pursuit of goals and aspirations with a clear sense of purpose.

1. Defining Your North Star: The Essence of Purpose

A Beacon in the Darkness

Explore the concept of purpose as your guiding light in the darkest moments. Understand how defining your north star brings clarity to your aspirations, aligning your actions with a higher calling that extends beyond personal gain.

2. Living with Intentionality

Delve into the art of intentional living, where every action is a deliberate step towards your purpose. Discover how cultivating a sense of intentionality infuses meaning into your daily activities, fostering a sense of fulfillment and accomplishment.

2. Aligning Goals with Purpose: The Strategic Approach

Strategic Goal Setting

Learn how to align your goals with your overarching purpose. Uncover the strategic approach to goal setting, ensuring that each objective contributes to the fulfillment of your higher calling outlined in Philippians 3:12-14.

3. Overcoming Obstacles with Purpose

Explore how purpose becomes a formidable force in overcoming obstacles. Discover strategies to navigate challenges with resilience, leveraging your sense of purpose as a source of motivation and determination.

3. Philippians Principles in Action: Case Studies

Embark on a journey through real-life case studies where individuals applied the principles of Philippians 3:12-14 to move forward with purpose. Witness how aligning actions with purpose transformed challenges into triumphs.

1. Career Advancement: A Purpose-Driven Approach

Explore case studies of individuals who advanced in their careers by aligning their professional goals with a sense of purpose. Learn from their strategies in navigating the corporate landscape with intentionality.

2. Personal Development: The Purposeful Path to Growth

Witness how purpose-driven personal development leads to transformative growth. These case studies illustrate how individuals cultivated a mindset of continuous learning and improvement in alignment with their higher calling.

Applying Purpose Across Domains

The chapter concludes by applying the principles of moving forward with purpose to various aspects of life, offering actionable insights for personal and professional development.

1. Purposeful Leadership

Explore the role of purpose in effective leadership. Understand how purpose-driven leaders inspire and motivate their teams, fostering a culture of excellence and shared vision.

2. Navigating Relationships with Purpose

Discover how purpose enhances the quality of relationships. Whether personal or professional, a sense of purpose contributes to more meaningful connections and collaborations.

3. Health and Wellness: A Purposeful Lifestyle

Embark on a purposeful journey towards health and wellness. Learn how aligning your wellness goals with a higher purpose creates a sustainable and fulfilling lifestyle.

Your Purpose Toolkit: Practical Strategies for Daily Application

As you conclude this chapter, find practical tools and exercises to integrate the principles of moving forward with purpose into your daily life. These tools will serve as your allies in cultivating a mindset that transforms aspirations into tangible achievements.

A Life Defined by Purpose

Chapter Four lays the groundwork for the subsequent chapters, setting the stage for a life characterized by intentionality, determination, and an unwavering commitment to purpose. As you embrace the teachings of Philippians 3:12-14, remember that your journey towards excellence is not a random walk but a purposeful stride towards a higher calling.

Move forward with purpose, and witness how each step becomes a testament to a life well-lived.

The Purposeful Journey: Unleashing Your Full Potential

In the symphony of life, purpose is the melody that orchestrates meaningful existence. This chapter dives deeper into the nuances of a purposeful journey, drawing inspiration from the timeless guidance of Philippians 3:12-14. Explore how every step becomes intentional, every decision purpose-driven, and witness the transformation that unfolds when your actions align with a higher calling.

1. Purpose as a Catalyst for Motivation

Uncover the inherent motivational power within purpose. Explore how a clear sense of purpose ignites a perpetual flame of motivation, fueling your endeavors with resilience and determination.

2. Living a Life of Significance

Dive into the concept of significance, where purpose infuses every action with meaning. Discover how aligning your actions with a higher calling elevates your sense of fulfillment, creating a life that resonates with purpose.

Philippians Principles in Action: Real-Life Narratives

Embark on a journey through real-life narratives that exemplify the principles of moving forward with purpose. These stories serve as beacons of inspiration, showcasing individuals who have harnessed the transformative power of purpose in various domains.

1. Professional Fulfillment: The Purposeful Career Path

Explore stories of individuals who found professional fulfillment by aligning their careers with a sense of purpose. Learn how a purpose-driven approach can turn a job into a vocation and transform the daily grind into a meaningful journey.

2. Personal Triumphs: The Impact of Purpose on Growth

Witness personal triumphs that emerged from a commitment to growth guided by purpose. These narratives demonstrate the resilience and determination that arise when personal development is grounded in a higher calling.

Aligning Purpose with Passion and Skills

Discover the intersection where purpose meets passion and skills. Understand how aligning your purpose with what you love and what you excel at creates a powerful synergy that propels you toward excellence.

1. Passion as the Compass of Purpose

Explore how passion becomes the compass that directs your purposeful journey. Uncover strategies for identifying and pursuing your passions in alignment with the higher calling outlined in Philippians 3:12-14.

2. Skills as Instruments of Purposeful Action

Delve into the role of skills as instruments in your purposeful toolkit. Learn how honing your skills in areas that resonate with your purpose amplifies the impact of your actions, creating a harmonious blend of passion, skills, and purpose.

Moving Forward with Purpose Across Life Domains

Apply the principles of moving forward with purpose to various domains, offering actionable insights for holistic personal and professional development.

1. Leadership: Guiding with Purpose

Explore how purposeful leadership shapes organizational culture. Learn from leaders who inspire and guide with a clear sense of purpose, fostering a workplace environment that values intentionality and shared vision.

2. Relationships: Building Meaningful Connections

Understand how purpose enhances the quality of relationships. Whether personal or professional, a sense of purpose contributes to deeper connections and collaborations, fostering a community driven by shared values.

3. Health and Wellness: A Purpose-Infused Lifestyle

Embark on a purpose-infused journey towards health and wellness. Discover how aligning wellness goals with a higher purpose creates a sustainable and fulfilling lifestyle.

Your Purpose Toolkit: Practical Strategies for Daily Application

Conclude this chapter with practical tools and exercises to integrate the principles of moving forward with purpose into your daily life. These tools will serve as your allies in cultivating a mindset that transforms aspirations into tangible achievements.

A Life of Purposeful Legacy

Chapter Four lays the groundwork for the subsequent chapters, setting the stage for a life characterized by intentionality, determination, and an unwavering commitment to purpose. As you embrace the teachings of Philippians 3:12-14, envision your journey as a purposeful stride towards a higher calling, leaving behind a legacy defined by the intentional pursuit of excellence.

Move forward with purpose, and witness how each step becomes a testament to a life well-lived, leaving an indelible mark on the world.

Chapter Five: Achieving Peak Performance through Focus

In the pursuit of excellence, the spotlight falls on achieving peak performance – a symphony of focus, dedication, and unwavering commitment. Rooted in the timeless wisdom of Philippians 3:12-14, this chapter unravels the secrets of channeling focus to reach unparalleled levels of performance. Brace yourself for insights, examples, and illustrations that will empower you to elevate your endeavors and achieve peak performance in every facet of life.

Philippians 3:12-14 as the Catalyst for Peak Performance

"Not that I have already obtained this or am already perfect, but I press on to make it my own because Christ Jesus has made me his own. Brothers, I do not consider that I have made it my own. But one thing I do: forgetting what lies behind and straining forward to what lies ahead, I press on toward the goal for the prize of the upward call of God in Christ Jesus." - Philippians 3:12-14 (ESV)

These verses serve as the foundation for achieving peak performance, emphasizing the focused pursuit of goals and aspirations.

1. The Art of Laser-Like Focus

Illustration: The Power of a Magnifying Glass

Imagine focus as a magnifying glass concentrating the sun's rays. Just as the focused sunlight can ignite a fire, laser-like focus intensifies your efforts, leading to extraordinary results. Learn strategies to cultivate and sustain this level of concentration.

Example: Elon Musk's Hyper-Focus

Explore how Elon Musk, the visionary entrepreneur, channels his focus with remarkable intensity. Musk's ability to immerse himself entirely in his projects showcases the transformative power of focused dedication, leading to groundbreaking innovations.

2. The Science of Flow State

Illustration: The River of Flow

Visualize the flow state as a river of optimal performance. When you immerse yourself in tasks that align with your skills and challenges, you enter the flow state, where focus is effortless, and peak performance becomes a natural outcome. Learn how to navigate this river of flow in various aspects of life.

Example: Michael Jordan's Legendary Focus

Delve into the career of Michael Jordan, whose unparalleled focus on the basketball court propelled him to legendary status. Jordan's ability to enter the flow state during crucial moments illustrates how focus can elevate performance to extraordinary heights.

3. Overcoming Distractions and Information Overload

Illustration: The Clarity of a Still Pond

Imagine your mind as a still pond, disturbed by distractions and information overload. Explore techniques to restore calmness and clarity to your mental pond, allowing for deeper focus and enhanced performance.

Example: Warren Buffett's Information Filtering

Learn from Warren Buffett's disciplined approach to information consumption. Buffett's ability to filter out unnecessary noise and focus on essential data showcases how selective attention contributes to sound decision-making and peak performance in the financial world.

4. Setting and Achieving Ambitious Goals

Illustration: The Summit of Everest

Envision your goals as the summit of Mount Everest. Climbing this metaphorical peak requires meticulous planning, unwavering focus, and relentless perseverance. Learn how to set ambitious yet attainable goals and navigate the challenging terrain towards peak performance.

Example: Sir Edmund Hillary and Tenzing Norgay's Everest Conquest

Explore the historic ascent of Mount Everest by Sir Edmund Hillary and Tenzing Norgay. Their focused determination to reach the summit illustrates the transformative power of setting and achieving ambitious goals.

5. Resilience in the Face of Challenges

Illustration: The Oak Tree in the Storm

Picture resilience as an oak tree standing tall in the midst of a storm. Challenges are inevitable, but with deep-rooted resilience, you can weather any adversity and continue the journey towards peak performance.

Example: Thomas Edison's Perseverance

Reflect on Thomas Edison's journey to invent the light bulb. Edison's relentless pursuit of success, despite numerous failures, demonstrates how resilience and unwavering focus lead to groundbreaking achievements.

Applying Peak Performance Principles Across Domains

Apply the principles of achieving peak performance to diverse areas of life, offering actionable insights for personal and professional development.

1. Career Mastery: Excelling in Your Profession

Discover strategies for achieving peak performance in your career. Whether you are an IT professional or pursuing any other profession, learn how focus can elevate your skills and contributions to new heights.

2. Personal Development: A Quest for Excellence

Explore how the principles of peak performance contribute to personal development. Uncover habits and practices that cultivate focus, ensuring continuous growth and excellence in various aspects of your life.

3. Relationships: Fostering Meaningful Connections

Understand the role of focus in building meaningful relationships. Explore how being present, attentive, and dedicated to fostering connections leads to richer and more fulfilling relationships.

Your Peak Performance Toolkit: Practical Strategies for Daily Application

As you conclude this chapter, find practical tools and exercises to integrate the principles of achieving peak performance into your daily life. These tools will serve as your allies in cultivating a mindset that propels you towards excellence in every endeavor.

The Peak Performance Mindset

Chapter Five lays the groundwork for the subsequent chapters, setting the stage for a life characterized by focus, dedication, and an unwavering commitment to achieving peak performance. As you embrace the teachings of Philippians 3:12-14, envision your journey as a relentless pursuit of excellence, where every action is infused with the transformative power of focused determination.

Achieve peak performance, and witness how each endeavor becomes a masterpiece of focused dedication, leaving an indelible mark on your path to extraordinary success.

Navigating the Peak: Strategies for Unmatched Performance

Embark on a journey to explore the intricate strategies that propel individuals toward unmatched performance. Drawing inspiration from Philippians 3:12-14, this chapter unveils the secrets to navigating the peak, where focus becomes the compass guiding you to unprecedented heights.

1. Mindfulness as the Gateway to Peak Focus

Visualize mindfulness as the gateway to peak focus. Delve into practices that bring you into the present moment, sharpening your concentration and enhancing your ability to perform at your best.

Illustration: The Archer's Concentrated Aim

Imagine an archer aiming at a target with unwavering focus. Learn how adopting a concentrated aim in your pursuits, akin to the archer, sharpens your focus and improves precision in every action.

Example: Steve Jobs' Mindfulness Practices

Explore how Steve Jobs, the visionary co-founder of Apple, embraced mindfulness practices. Jobs' commitment to meditation and present-moment awareness highlights the impact of mindfulness on creativity, decision-making, and sustained peak performance.

2. The Role of Passion in Sustaining Focus

Understand the symbiotic relationship between passion and sustained focus. Visualize passion as the fuel that keeps the fire of focus burning, propelling you forward with unwavering determination.

Illustration: The Sailboat and Wind of Passion

Envision your passion as the wind filling the sails of a sailboat. Learn how the alignment of your actions with your passion propels you forward, navigating challenges with grace and purpose.

Example: Serena Williams' Passion for Tennis

Witness how Serena Williams' passion for tennis fueled her unparalleled success. Williams' unwavering dedication to her sport illustrates the transformative power of aligning passion with focused determination.

3. Mastering Time Management for Optimal Focus

Dive into the art of mastering time management to optimize your focus. Visualize time as a precious resource, and explore strategies to allocate it effectively, ensuring that your efforts lead to peak performance.

Illustration: The Conductor's Precision in Timing

Picture a conductor leading an orchestra with precision in timing. Learn how adopting a conductor's mindset in managing your time orchestrates harmony in your activities, allowing for focused, peak performance.

Example: Elon Musk's Time Blocking Technique

Explore Elon Musk's time blocking technique as an example of effective time management. Musk's disciplined approach to structuring his day showcases how strategic allocation of time enhances focus and productivity.

4. Leveraging Technology for Enhanced Focus

Uncover the ways in which technology can be harnessed to enhance focus and performance. Visualize technology as a tool that, when used mindfully, amplifies your capabilities and accelerates your journey toward the peak.

Illustration: The Precision of a Surgeon's Scalpel

Imagine a surgeon's precision using a scalpel, representing the focused use of technology. Learn how incorporating technology mindfully, like a surgeon's precision, sharpens your skills and facilitates peak performance.

Example: Jeff Bezos' Tech-Driven Focus at Amazon

Discover how Jeff Bezos leveraged technology to drive focus and efficiency at Amazon. Bezos' innovative use of technology transformed Amazon into a global powerhouse, showcasing the potential of integrating technology for unmatched performance.

Applying Peak Performance to Diverse Life Domains

Apply the principles of achieving peak performance to diverse areas of life, offering actionable insights for comprehensive personal and professional development.

1. Career Excellence: Strategies for IT Professionals

Explore strategies for achieving peak performance in the field of IT. Learn how focus, passion, and effective time management contribute to excellence in your career as an IT professional.

2. Personal Growth: Cultivating Peak Performance Habits

Delve into habits and practices that foster personal growth and peak performance. Uncover how aligning your actions with a purpose-driven focus accelerates your journey toward continuous improvement.

3. Interpersonal Relationships: The Art of Focused Connection

Understand how focus enhances the quality of interpersonal relationships. Explore ways to be present and attentive, fostering deeper connections with others and enriching the fabric of your social life.

Your Peak Performance Toolkit: Practical Strategies for Daily Application

As you conclude this chapter, discover practical tools and exercises to integrate the principles of achieving peak performance into your daily life. These tools will serve as your allies in cultivating a mindset that propels you toward excellence in every endeavor.

The Summit Beckons

Chapter Five sets the stage for a life characterized by focus, dedication, and an unwavering commitment to achieving peak performance. As you embrace the teachings of Philippians 3:12-14, envision your journey as a relentless pursuit of excellence, where every action is infused with the transformative power of focused determination.

Navigate the peak with purpose and passion, and witness how each step becomes a testament to a life lived at the summit of unparalleled success.

Chapter Six: Forging Resilience in Adversity

In the crucible of life's challenges, resilience emerges as the crucible that transforms adversity into opportunity. Rooted in the timeless wisdom of Philippians 3:12-14, this chapter unveils the art of forging resilience, empowering you to navigate storms with unwavering strength and emerge stronger on the other side. Brace yourself for insights, examples, and illustrations that will not only inspire but equip you with the tools to forge an unbreakable spirit in the face of adversity.

Philippians 3:12-14 as the Anvil of Resilience

"Not that I have already obtained this or am already perfect, but I press on to make it my own because Christ Jesus has made me his own. Brothers, I do not consider that I have made it my own. But one thing I do: forgetting what lies behind and straining forward to what lies ahead, I press on toward the goal for the prize of the upward call of God in Christ Jesus." - Philippians 3:12-14 (ESV)

These verses serve as the anvil upon which resilience is forged, emphasizing the continual pursuit of goals despite obstacles.

1. The Phoenix Rising: Resilience as Transformation

Illustration: The Phoenix Rebirth

Imagine resilience as the mythical phoenix, rising from the ashes of adversity. Explore how every challenge becomes an opportunity for transformation, allowing you to emerge stronger and more resilient than before.

Example: Nelson Mandela's Triumph Over Adversity

Delve into Nelson Mandela's life as an example of resilience. Mandela's ability to endure decades of imprisonment and emerge as a symbol of reconciliation showcases the transformative power of resilience in the face of profound adversity.

2. The Elasticity of the Human Spirit

Illustration: The Rubber Band

Picture the human spirit as a resilient rubber band. Learn how cultivating resilience allows you to stretch beyond your perceived limits, bouncing back from setbacks with newfound strength and flexibility.

Example: J.K. Rowling's Literary Resilience

Explore J.K. Rowling's journey to literary success. Rowling faced numerous rejections before the publication of Harry Potter. Her unwavering commitment to her craft exemplifies the resilience needed to overcome adversity and achieve extraordinary success.

3. Embracing Setbacks as Setups for Comebacks

Illustration: The Springboard

Visualize setbacks as springboards that propel you toward comebacks. Understand how a resilient mindset transforms setbacks into opportunities for growth and eventual triumph.

Example: Walt Disney's Animated Resilience

Uncover Walt Disney's story of resilience in the face of business failures and setbacks. Disney's ability to turn adversity into innovation led to the creation of a global entertainment empire, illustrating the potential of bouncing back from setbacks.

4. The Power of Positive Affirmations in Resilience Building

Illustration: The Mirror of Affirmations

Envision positive affirmations as a mirror reflecting your inner resilience. Explore how affirming your strengths and capabilities fortifies your mindset, enabling you to face challenges with courage and resilience.

Example: Serena Williams' Affirmative Resilience

Witness Serena Williams' use of positive affirmations to overcome challenges on and off the tennis court. Williams' mental resilience, strengthened by affirmations, illustrates the impact of a positive mindset in the face of adversity.

5. Cultivating a Growth Mindset for Resilience

Illustration: The Blooming Garden

Picture a growth mindset as a garden, where resilience acts as the fertile soil. Delve into how cultivating a mindset that embraces challenges as opportunities for growth fosters enduring resilience.

Example: Thomas Edison's Growth-Oriented Resilience

Explore Thomas Edison's relentless pursuit of innovation. Edison's countless failures were viewed not as defeats but as steps towards success, showcasing the resilience embedded in a growth-oriented mindset.

Applying Resilience Principles Across Life Domains

Apply the principles of forging resilience to various areas of life, offering actionable insights for personal and professional development.

1. Career Resilience: Navigating Professional Challenges

Discover strategies for cultivating resilience in your career. Learn how to navigate professional challenges with a resilient mindset, turning setbacks into steppingstones for advancement.

2. Personal Resilience: Thriving in Personal Turbulence

Explore ways to foster personal resilience amidst life's turbulence. Uncover practices that enhance your ability to adapt, grow, and thrive, even in the face of personal challenges.

3. Interpersonal Resilience: Building Strong Connections

Understand how resilience enhances the quality of interpersonal relationships. Explore strategies to navigate conflicts, setbacks, and misunderstandings with resilience, fostering stronger and more authentic connections.

Your Resilience Toolkit: Practical Strategies for Daily Application

As you conclude this chapter, discover practical tools and exercises to integrate the principles of forging resilience into your daily life. These tools will serve as your allies in cultivating a mindset that not only withstands adversity but transforms it into a catalyst for growth and success.

An Unbreakable Spirit

Chapter Six sets the stage for a life characterized by resilience, an unbreakable spirit forged in the fires of adversity. As you embrace the teachings of Philippians 3:12-14, envision your journey as a testament to the transformative power of resilience, where challenges become steppingstones toward an extraordinary life.

Forge resilience, and witness how each trial becomes an opportunity to rise, stronger and more resilient, in the pursuit of your goals and aspirations.

The Resilient Journey: Triumph in Adversity

Journey deeper into the realm of resilience, where adversities become steppingstones to triumph. In this chapter, inspired by Philippians 3:12-14, explores the intricacies of cultivating an unyielding spirit that not only weathers the storm but transforms challenges into opportunities for growth and triumph.

1. Resilience as a Navigation System

Illustration: The Lighthouse in the Storm

Envision resilience as a lighthouse guiding you through the stormy seas of life. Delve into how developing resilience serves as a reliable navigation system, allowing you to stay on course even amidst turbulent waters.

Example: Oprah Winfrey's Resilient Navigation

Explore Oprah Winfrey's journey as a testament to resilient navigation. Winfrey faced adversities throughout her life, from a challenging childhood to professional setbacks, yet she navigated through challenges to become a media mogul and philanthropist.

2. The Dance of Resilience and Adaptability

Illustration: The Dance of the Bamboo in the Wind

Picture resilience as the flexibility of bamboo swaying in the wind. Understand how resilience and adaptability dance together, allowing you to bend without breaking in the face of life's gusts.

Example: Charles Darwin's Adaptive Resilience

Dive into the life of Charles Darwin, who not only introduced the theory of evolution but exemplified adaptive resilience. Darwin's ability to adapt to changing circumstances and challenges laid the foundation for scientific progress.

3. Turning Setbacks into Comebacks: The Resilient Narrative

Illustration: The Phoenix Soaring Again

Imagine setbacks as the embers from which the phoenix of resilience rises. Explore how crafting a resilient narrative turns setbacks into powerful comebacks, rewriting the story of your journey.

Example: Malala Yousafzai's Resilient Narrative

Discover Malala Yousafzai's resilient narrative. Despite facing violence and oppression for advocating education for girls, Malala emerged stronger, becoming a global advocate for education and the youngest Nobel Prize laureate.

4. Emotional Resilience: The Heart's Armor

Illustration: The Armor of a Warrior's Heart

Visualize emotional resilience as the armor protecting your heart. Uncover how developing emotional resilience shields you from the impact of hardships, allowing you to face challenges with a steadfast heart.

Example: Viktor Frankl's Heartfelt Resilience

Explore the profound emotional resilience of Viktor Frankl, a Holocaust survivor and psychiatrist. Frankl's ability to find meaning in suffering showcases the resilience of the human spirit even in the darkest of times.

5. Resilience in Decision-Making: Navigating Crossroads

Illustration: The Compass in Decision-Making

Picture resilience as a compass guiding your decisions through crossroads. Examine how resilience influences decision-making, helping you make choices that align with your goals even in the face of uncertainty.

Example: Sheryl Sandberg's Decisional Resilience

Delve into Sheryl Sandberg's decisional resilience. In the aftermath of personal tragedy, Sandberg exemplified resilience in decision-making, demonstrating strength and determination in the face of adversity.

Applying Resilience Across Life Domains

Apply the principles of resilience to various domains of life, offering actionable insights for holistic personal and professional development.

1. Career Resilience: Thriving Amidst Professional Challenges

Explore strategies for building resilience in your career. Learn how to navigate professional challenges with a resilient mindset, fostering not only survival but growth and success.

2. Personal Resilience: Flourishing in Life's Mosaic

Uncover practices that foster personal resilience amidst life's mosaic of experiences. Learn to embrace challenges as opportunities for personal growth, creating a resilient foundation for an enriching life.

3. Interpersonal Resilience: Strengthening Bonds Through Challenges

Understand how resilience enhances the quality of interpersonal relationships. Explore strategies to navigate conflicts and setbacks with resilience, fostering stronger and more authentic connections.

Your Resilience Toolkit: Practical Strategies for Daily Application

As you conclude this chapter, discover practical tools and exercises to integrate the principles of resilience into your daily life. These tools will serve as your allies in cultivating a mindset that not only withstands adversity but transforms it into a catalyst for growth and success.

The Resilient Symphony

Chapter Six sets the stage for a life characterized by resilience – a symphony of triumph in adversity. As you embrace the teachings of Philippians 3:12-14, envision your journey as a testament to the transformative power of resilience, where challenges become steppingstones toward an extraordinary life.

Forge resilience, dance with adaptability, and let the symphony of triumph echo through each chapter of your life, leaving an indelible mark on your path to extraordinary success.

Chapter Seven: Philippians Approach to Career Success

———

In the pursuit of a successful and fulfilling career, the wisdom encapsulated in Philippians 3:12-14 serves as a guiding light. This chapter unveils the Philippians approach to career success, where continuous growth, purposeful focus, and unwavering determination converge to create a blueprint for unparalleled professional achievement. Let the principles from Philippians infuse your career with purpose and propel you toward extraordinary success.

Philippians 3:12-14: Navigating the Professional Path

"Not that I have already obtained this or am already perfect, but I press on to make it my own because Christ Jesus has made me his own. Brothers, I do not consider that I have made it my own. But one thing I do: forgetting what lies behind and straining forward to what lies ahead, I press on toward the goal for the prize of the upward call of God in Christ Jesus." - Philippians 3:12-14 (ESV)

This passage becomes the compass for your career journey, emphasizing continual growth, purposeful focus, and an unwavering commitment to your professional goals.

1. The Journey of Continuous Learning

Embark on a journey of continuous learning, where each experience, success, or setback becomes a steppingstone for growth. Discover the transformative power of adopting a mindset that views learning as a perpetual and essential companion on your career path.

Example: Satya Nadella's Growth Mindset

Explore Satya Nadella's leadership journey at Microsoft. Nadella's commitment to continuous learning and his transformative approach revitalized Microsoft, showcasing the impact of a growth mindset on career success.

2. Purpose-Driven Professionalism

Infuse purpose into your professional endeavors, aligning your career with a higher calling that transcends mere success. Uncover the transformative power of combining your skills and passion with a sense of purpose, creating a fulfilling and impactful career.

Example: Tim Cook's Purpose-Infused Leadership

Dive into Tim Cook's leadership at Apple, where purpose plays a central role. Cook's commitment to sustainability, social responsibility, and innovation exemplifies how aligning your career with a higher purpose enhances professional success.

3. Unwavering Focus on Goals

Cultivate a Philippians-inspired focus on your career goals, where each step is intentional and guided by a clear vision. Explore strategies to overcome distractions, maintain laser-like focus, and translate your aspirations into tangible achievements.

Example: Jeff Bezos' Visionary Focus at Amazon

Delve into Jeff Bezos' visionary focus in building Amazon. Bezos' unwavering commitment to long-term goals and customer-centric innovation illustrates the impact of sustained focus on achieving unprecedented success.

4. Resilience in Professional Challenges

Forge resilience as an armor against the inevitable challenges in your professional journey. Discover how setbacks can become catalysts for growth and success and cultivate the strength to endure and triumph in the face of adversity.

Example: Oprah Winfrey's Resilience in Media

Explore Oprah Winfrey's media career, marked by resilience in the face of obstacles. Oprah's ability to overcome challenges and build an influential media empire showcases the transformative power of resilience in achieving lasting success.

5. Building Meaningful Professional Connections

Recognize the importance of meaningful professional relationships in your career. Discover how fostering genuine connections, collaboration, and mentorship can amplify your professional growth and contribute to a fulfilling career journey.

Example: Warren Buffett's Relationship-Centric Success

Learn from Warren Buffett's approach to professional relationships. Buffett's emphasis on integrity, trust, and long-term partnerships underscores the value of meaningful connections in achieving sustained career success.

Applying Philippians Principles Across Career Domains

Apply the principles derived from Philippians to diverse career domains, offering actionable insights for comprehensive professional development.

1. IT Professional Excellence: A Philippians-Driven Approach

Explore strategies for achieving excellence as an IT professional. Learn how the Philippians approach to continuous learning, purpose-driven professionalism, and unwavering focus can elevate your skills and contributions.

2. Entrepreneurial Success: Philippians Principles for Startups

Delve into how entrepreneurs can apply Philippians principles to build successful startups. Explore the importance of purpose, continuous learning, focus, and resilience in navigating the challenges of entrepreneurship.

3. Corporate Leadership: Guiding with Philippians Values

Understand how corporate leaders can embody Philippians values in their leadership style. Explore the impact of purpose-driven leadership, continuous learning, focused goal-setting, and resilience on shaping successful organizations.

Your Philippians Career Toolkit: Practical Strategies for Daily Application

As you conclude this chapter, discover practical tools and exercises to integrate the Philippians approach into your daily professional life. These tools will serve as your allies in cultivating a career mindset grounded in continuous growth, purposeful focus, and unwavering determination.

The Philippians Professional Symphony

Chapter Seven sets the stage for a career characterized by continuous growth, purpose-driven focus, and unwavering determination—a symphony of success inspired by Philippians 3:12-14. As you embrace this approach, envision your professional journey as a testament to the transformative power of aligning your career with timeless principles, leaving an indelible mark on the world through your professional achievements.

Forge a Philippians-inspired career, and witness how each step becomes a harmonious note in the symphony of your professional success.

Chapter Eight: Cultivating Meaningful Relationships

In the intricate tapestry of life, relationships form the threads that weave our experiences. Rooted in the timeless wisdom of Philippians 3:12-14, this chapter unravels the art of cultivating meaningful relationships. Embrace the transformative power of building connections that enrich your journey, embodying the essence of continuous growth, purposeful focus, and unwavering commitment to others.

Philippians 3:12-14: A Blueprint for Meaningful Connections

"Not that I have already obtained this or am already perfect, but I press on to make it my own because Christ Jesus has made me his own. Brothers, I do not consider that I have made it my own. But one thing I do: forgetting what lies behind and straining forward to what lies ahead, I press on toward the goal for the prize of the upward call of God in Christ Jesus." - Philippians 3:12-14 (ESV)

Let these verses guide your approach to relationships, fostering an environment of growth, purpose, and unwavering commitment.

1. Authentic Connections: Embracing Your True Self

Embark on a journey of authenticity in your relationships, where vulnerability becomes the bridge to genuine connections. Explore how embracing your true self and allowing others to do the same creates a foundation for meaningful and lasting relationships.

Example: Brené Brown's Authentic Vulnerability

Delve into Brené Brown's work on vulnerability. Brown's research emphasizes the transformative power of authenticity, showing how embracing vulnerability fosters deep connections and genuine relationships.

2. The Art of Active Listening

Cultivate the art of active listening as a cornerstone of meaningful relationships. Discover how being fully present and engaged in conversations fosters understanding, empathy, and a sense of connection with those around you.

Example: Oprah Winfrey's Empathetic Listening

Explore Oprah Winfrey's empathetic listening skills. Oprah's ability to actively listen and connect with her guests demonstrates how this fundamental practice enriches relationships and contributes to personal growth.

3. Purposeful Relationships: Aligning Values and Goals

Align your relationships with a sense of purpose, connecting with individuals who share similar values and aspirations. Explore how purposeful connections contribute to mutual growth, support, and the fulfillment of shared goals.

Example: Bill and Melinda Gates' Philanthropic Partnership

Dive into the philanthropic partnership of Bill and Melinda Gates. Their shared purpose of addressing global challenges through their foundation illustrates how aligning values and goals fosters meaningful and impactful relationships.

4. Nurturing Family Bonds: A Foundation of Support

Recognize the importance of nurturing family bonds as a foundation for meaningful relationships. Explore how family connections, rooted in love and support, provide a resilient network that contributes to personal and professional well-being.

Example: The Obamas' Family Values

Reflect on the Obamas' commitment to family values. Barack and Michelle Obama's prioritization of family and their strong bond with their daughters showcase how family relationships can be a source of strength and inspiration.

5. Giving and Receiving: The Reciprocity of Relationships

Understand the reciprocity inherent in meaningful relationships, where both giving and receiving contribute to the richness of connections. Explore how acts of kindness, support, and generosity create a harmonious exchange within your social circles.

Example: Warren Buffett's Generosity

Learn from Warren Buffett's philanthropic endeavors. Buffett's commitment to giving back to society exemplifies the transformative impact of generosity on building meaningful relationships and contributing to the greater good.

Applying Philippians Principles Across Relationship Domains

Apply the principles derived from Philippians to various relationship domains, offering actionable insights for comprehensive personal and social development.

1. Friendship Dynamics: Building Lifelong Bonds

Explore strategies for building and maintaining meaningful friendships. Learn how the Philippians approach to authenticity, active listening, purpose, and reciprocity enhances the quality of your friendships.

2. Romantic Relationships: Nurturing Love and Connection

Delve into the dynamics of romantic relationships guided by Philippians principles. Explore how authenticity, shared purpose, and reciprocity contribute to the growth and longevity of meaningful romantic connections.

3. Professional Networks: Creating a Supportive Community

Understand how the Philippians approach applies to professional networks. Explore strategies for building a supportive community, where shared values and goals contribute to professional growth and success.

Your Relationship Toolkit: Practical Strategies for Daily Application

As you conclude this chapter, discover practical tools and exercises to integrate the Philippians approach into your daily life. These tools will serve as your allies in cultivating a mindset that not only values meaningful connections but actively contributes to the growth and fulfillment of those around you.

The Tapestry of Meaningful Connections

Chapter Eight sets the stage for a life characterized by meaningful relationships—a tapestry woven with threads of authenticity, active listening, purpose, and reciprocity. As you embrace the teachings of Philippians 3:12-14, envision your relationships as a testament to the transformative power of aligning connections with timeless principles, leaving an indelible mark on the world through the depth and impact of your relationships.

Cultivate meaningful connections, and witness how each relationship becomes a vibrant thread, contributing to the beautiful tapestry of your life.

Chapter Nine: Fitness and Focus: A Holistic Approach

———

In the pursuit of excellence and fulfillment, nurturing both body and mind forms the cornerstone of a holistic approach to life. Inspired by the timeless wisdom of Philippians 3:12-14, this chapter explores the symbiotic relationship between fitness and focus. Embrace the transformative power of aligning physical wellness with mental clarity, embodying the essence of continuous growth, purposeful focus, and unwavering commitment to holistic well-being.

Philippians 3:12-14: A Call to Holistic Wellness

"Not that I have already obtained this or am already perfect, but I press on to make it my own because Christ Jesus has made me his own. Brothers, I do not consider that I have made it my own. But one thing I do: forgetting what lies behind and straining forward to what lies ahead, I press on toward the goal for the prize of the upward call of God in Christ Jesus." - Philippians 3:12-14 (ESV)

Let these verses inspire your journey toward holistic wellness, where physical fitness and mental focus converge to empower your pursuit of excellence.

1. The Mind-Body Connection: Nurturing Harmony

Explore the intricate connection between mind and body, were physical vitality fuels mental acuity and vice versa. Understand how nurturing harmony between body and mind lays the foundation for holistic well-being and optimal performance.

Example: LeBron James' Mind-Body Synergy

Witness LeBron James' dedication to holistic wellness. James' commitment to physical fitness, coupled with mental focus and mindfulness practices, illustrates the transformative power of nurturing the mind-body connection.

2. Fitness as a Catalyst for Mental Clarity

Discover how physical fitness serves as a catalyst for mental clarity and focus. Explore the profound impact of regular exercise on cognitive function, stress management, and overall mental well-being.

Example: Serena Williams' Fitness-Mindfulness Fusion

Learn from Serena Williams' integration of fitness and mindfulness. Williams' rigorous training regimen, complemented by mindfulness practices such as yoga and meditation, underscores the synergy between physical vitality and mental clarity.

3. Cultivating Discipline Through Exercise

Delve into the discipline cultivated through exercise, where consistency, perseverance, and goal setting become guiding principles. Uncover how the discipline fostered in physical fitness transcends into other areas of life, nurturing a mindset of focused determination.

Example: Usain Bolt's Discipline in Training

Explore Usain Bolt's disciplined approach to training. Bolt's relentless pursuit of excellence in track and field exemplifies how discipline cultivated through exercise propels individuals toward unparalleled achievements.

4. Mindfulness in Movement: Finding Flow

Embrace mindfulness in movement as a pathway to finding flow—a state of effortless focus and immersion in the present moment.

Discover how activities such as yoga, tai chi, and mindful walking cultivate mental clarity and inner peace.

Example: Novak Djokovic's Mindful Tennis Mastery

Witness Novak Djokovic's mastery of mindfulness in tennis. Djokovic's ability to maintain focus and composure during high-pressure matches showcases the transformative power of mindfulness in optimizing performance.

5. Nutrition: Fueling Body and Mind

Understand the importance of nutrition in fueling both body and mind. Explore how a balanced diet rich in nutrients enhances physical vitality, cognitive function, and overall well-being, providing the foundation for sustained focus and energy.

Example: Tom Brady's Nutritional Excellence

Learn from Tom Brady's commitment to nutritional excellence. Brady's emphasis on a plant-based diet and nutrient-dense foods highlights the profound impact of nutrition on physical performance and mental clarity.

Applying Philippians Principles to Fitness and Focus

Apply the principles derived from Philippians to your fitness and focus journey, offering actionable insights for comprehensive well-being.

1. Exercise Habits: Building Consistency and Purpose

Explore strategies for cultivating exercise habits aligned with your goals and values. Learn how the Philippians approach to discipline and focus enhances consistency and purpose in your fitness regimen.

2. Mindfulness Practices: Cultivating Presence and Awareness

Delve into mindfulness practices that cultivate presence and awareness in your daily life. Discover how incorporating mindfulness into your routine nurtures mental clarity, resilience, and emotional balance.

3. Nutrition Strategies: Nourishing Body and Mind

Understand the principles of nutrition that nourish both body and mind. Explore how mindful eating, balanced macronutrient intake, and hydration optimize physical vitality and cognitive function.

Your Holistic Wellness Toolkit: Practical Strategies for Daily Application

As you conclude this chapter, discover practical tools and exercises to integrate the Philippians approach to fitness and focus into your daily life. These tools will serve as your allies in cultivating a lifestyle that prioritizes holistic well-being and empowers your pursuit of excellence.

The Holistic Pursuit of Excellence

Chapter Nine sets the stage for a life characterized by holistic wellness—a journey where fitness and focus converge to empower your pursuit of excellence. As you embrace the teachings of Philippians 3:12-14, envision your path as a testament to the transformative power of aligning physical vitality with mental clarity, leaving an indelible mark on the world through your holistic well-being.

Cultivate fitness, nurture focus, and witness how the synergy between body and mind propels you toward unparalleled achievements and fulfillment.

Chapter Ten: Financial Mastery with Philippians Wisdom

In the pursuit of a prosperous and purposeful life, the wisdom encapsulated in Philippians 3:12-14 becomes a guiding beacon for financial mastery. This chapter explores the intersection of Philippians principles with financial well-being, emphasizing continuous growth, purposeful focus, and unwavering commitment to financial success. Enrich your financial journey with the transformative power of aligning your financial goals with timeless principles.

Philippians 3:12-14: A Blueprint for Financial Abundance

"Not that I have already obtained this or am already perfect, but I press on to make it my own because Christ Jesus has made me his own. Brothers, I do not consider that I have made it my own. But one thing I do: forgetting what lies behind and straining forward to what lies ahead, I press on toward the goal for the prize of the upward call of God in Christ Jesus." - Philippians 3:12-14 (ESV)

Allow these verses to guide your financial journey, where continuous growth, purposeful focus, and unwavering commitment shape a path toward financial abundance.

1. Stewardship and Purposeful Wealth

Explore the concept of financial stewardship guided by purpose. Understand how aligning your financial decisions with your values and life purpose transforms wealth into a tool for positive impact and fulfillment.

Example: Warren Buffett's Philanthropic Stewardship

Delve into Warren Buffett's approach to financial stewardship. Buffett's commitment to philanthropy and responsible financial management exemplifies how purposeful wealth can create a lasting impact on individuals and communities.

2. The Power of Financial Focus

Cultivate financial focus by aligning your resources with your long-term goals. Explore strategies for maintaining clarity amidst financial complexities, allowing you to navigate challenges and make informed decisions.

Example: Elon Musk's Focus on Innovation

Learn from Elon Musk's financial focus on innovation. Musk's strategic approach to investments and dedication to transformative technologies showcases how financial focus can lead to groundbreaking success.

3. Investing for Long-Term Growth

Understand the principles of investing for long-term growth, where patience, strategic planning, and a focus on fundamentals become key elements. Explore how adopting an investor mindset rooted in continuous learning and discipline can lead to financial success.

Example: Charlie Munger's Investment Philosophy

Delve into Charlie Munger's investment philosophy. Munger's emphasis on rationality, patience, and a focus on long-term value creation provides insights into the mindset needed for sustainable financial growth.

4. Financial Resilience in Adversity

Forge financial resilience by adopting a mindset that transforms setbacks into opportunities for growth. Explore strategies for building financial resilience, allowing you to weather economic uncertainties and emerge stronger.

Example: Oprah Winfrey's Financial Resilience

Explore Oprah Winfrey's journey to financial resilience. Oprah's ability to overcome financial challenges and build a media empire demonstrates the transformative power of resilience in achieving lasting financial success.

5. Generosity and Philanthropy: The Wealth of Giving

Understand the wealth of giving by incorporating generosity and philanthropy into your financial journey. Explore how contributing to causes greater than oneself not only makes a positive impact on society but also enhances personal fulfillment.

Example: Bill and Melinda Gates' Philanthropic Legacy

Dive into the philanthropic legacy of Bill and Melinda Gates. Their commitment to addressing global challenges through the Gates Foundation illustrates how generosity and philanthropy can be integral components of financial mastery.

Applying Philippians Principles to Financial Success

Apply the principles derived from Philippians to your financial journey, offering actionable insights for comprehensive financial well-being.

1. Budgeting with Purpose: Aligning Finances with Values

Explore strategies for budgeting with purpose, aligning your financial decisions with your values and goals. Learn how Philippians principles guide purposeful financial planning and management.

2. Investment Mindset: Navigating Markets with Wisdom

Delve into the mindset of successful investing, where continuous learning, discipline, and a focus on long-term goals drive financial decisions. Discover how Philippians wisdom can shape a resilient and growth-oriented investment approach.

3. Financial Planning for Life Goals: A Philippians Roadmap

Understand how financial planning a roadmap can be achieving life goals. Explore the integration of Philippians principles into financial planning, fostering a holistic approach that aligns financial success with overall well-being.

Your Financial Mastery Toolkit: Practical Strategies for Daily Application

As you conclude this chapter, discover practical tools and exercises to integrate the Philippians approach to financial mastery into your daily life. These tools will serve as your allies in cultivating a financial mindset grounded in continuous growth, purposeful focus, and unwavering commitment.

A Financial Legacy of Purpose

Chapter Ten sets the stage for a financial life characterized by purposeful abundance—a journey where continuous growth, purposeful focus, and unwavering commitment converge to empower your pursuit of financial success. As you embrace the teachings of Philippians 3:12-14, envision your financial legacy as a testament to the transformative power of aligning your wealth with timeless principles.

Chapter Eleven: Education: Focused Learning for Lifelong Success

In the pursuit of knowledge and personal development, education emerges as a cornerstone for lifelong success. Guided by the wisdom encapsulated in Philippians 3:12-14, this chapter explores the transformative power of focused learning. Embrace the journey of continuous growth, purposeful focus, and unwavering commitment to education as a catalyst for personal and professional excellence.

Philippians 3:12-14: A Pathway to Enlightened Learning

"Not that I have already obtained this or am already perfect, but I press on to make it my own because Christ Jesus has made me his own. Brothers, I do not consider that I have made it my own. But one thing I do: forgetting what lies behind and straining forward to what lies ahead, I press on toward the goal for the prize of the upward call of God in Christ Jesus." - Philippians 3:12-14 (ESV)

Allow these verses to guide your educational journey, where continuous growth, purposeful focus, and unwavering commitment converge to empower your pursuit of knowledge.

1. Lifelong Learning: The Essence of Growth

Embrace the concept of lifelong learning, where each moment becomes an opportunity for intellectual growth. Explore how adopting a mindset of continuous learning contributes to personal and professional excellence.

Example: Elon Musk's Insatiable Curiosity

Witness Elon Musk's commitment to lifelong learning. Musk's curiosity-driven approach to learning spans various disciplines, showcasing the transformative power of continuous intellectual exploration.

2. Purpose-Driven Education

Align your educational pursuits with a sense of purpose, connecting learning with your broader life goals. Explore how purposeful education not only enhances your knowledge but also propels you toward a fulfilling and impactful life.

Example: Malala Yousafzai's Educational Advocacy

Delve into Malala Yousafzai's advocacy for purposeful education. Malala's commitment to girls' education reflects the transformative impact of aligning educational endeavors with a higher purpose.

3. Focused Study Habits

Cultivate focused study habits that optimize your learning experience. Explore strategies for maintaining concentration, managing distractions, and immersing yourself in the material, fostering a purposeful and efficient learning journey.

Example: Bill Gates' Strategic Reading Habits

Learn from Bill Gates' approach to focused learning. Gates' strategic reading habits and dedication to in-depth understanding showcase the power of focused study in acquiring profound knowledge.

4. Learning from Setbacks: Resilience in Education

Forge resilience in the face of academic challenges, viewing setbacks as opportunities for growth. Explore how adopting a resilient mindset in education empowers you to overcome obstacles and emerge stronger.

Example: J.K. Rowling's Journey of Perseverance

Dive into J.K. Rowling's journey of resilience in education. Rowling's challenges and setbacks ultimately fueled her determination to become a successful author, illustrating the transformative power of perseverance in learning.

5. Embracing Diverse Learning Modalities

Recognize the value of diverse learning modalities that cater to different styles and preferences. Explore how incorporating a variety of learning methods enhances comprehension, retention, and overall educational effectiveness.

Example: Sir Ken Robinson's Advocacy for Creative Learning

Explore Sir Ken Robinson's advocacy for creative and diverse learning. Robinson's emphasis on fostering creativity in education highlights the importance of embracing varied modalities for a comprehensive learning experience.

Applying Philippians Principles to Educational Excellence

Apply the principles derived from Philippians to your educational journey, offering actionable insights for comprehensive personal and intellectual development.

1. Goal-Oriented Learning: Aligning Education with Life Objectives

Explore strategies for aligning your education with broader life objectives. Learn how the Philippians approach to purposeful focus contributes to goal-oriented learning and the pursuit of meaningful knowledge.

2. Continuous Skill Development: A Philippians Mindset

Delve into the continuous development of skills guided by a Philippians mindset. Explore how acquiring new skills and refining existing ones contributes to intellectual growth and adaptability in an ever-evolving world.

3. Educational Resilience: Navigating Academic Challenges

Understand how the principles of resilience apply to education. Explore strategies for navigating academic challenges with determination, embracing setbacks as opportunities for learning and personal development.

Your Educational Mastery Toolkit: Practical Strategies for Daily Application

As you conclude this chapter, discover practical tools and exercises to integrate the Philippians approach to focused learning into your daily life. These tools will serve as your allies in cultivating an educational mindset grounded in continuous growth, purposeful focus, and unwavering commitment.

The Enlightened Scholar's Journey

Chapter Eleven sets the stage for an educational journey characterized by focused learning—a voyage where continuous growth, purposeful focus, and unwavering commitment converge to empower your pursuit of knowledge. As you embrace the teachings of Philippians 3:12-14, envision your educational path as a testament to the transformative power of aligning your learning endeavors with timeless principles, leaving an indelible mark on the world through your intellectual contributions.

Chapter Twelve: Entrepreneurial Excellence through Philippians Principles

———

Embark on a journey of entrepreneurial excellence guided by the timeless wisdom of Philippians 3:12-14. In this chapter, explore the transformative power of aligning entrepreneurial pursuits with continuous growth, purposeful focus, and unwavering commitment. Navigate the dynamic landscape of business with a mindset grounded in Philippians principles, fostering a path to success that transcends traditional measures.

Philippians 3:12-14: A Blueprint for Entrepreneurial Triumph

"Not that I have already obtained this or am already perfect, but I press on to make it my own because Christ Jesus has made me his own. Brothers, I do not consider that I have made it my own. But one thing I do: forgetting what lies behind and straining forward to what lies ahead, I press on toward the goal for the prize of the upward call of God in Christ Jesus." - Philippians 3:12-14 (ESV)

Allow these verses to guide your entrepreneurial journey, where continuous growth, purposeful focus, and unwavering commitment converge to empower your pursuit of business excellence.

1. Visionary Leadership: A Philippians Perspective

Embrace visionary leadership rooted in Philippians principles, where a clear vision becomes the driving force behind entrepreneurial endeavors. Explore how aligning your leadership with a higher purpose propels your team toward shared goals and impactful success.

Example: Steve Jobs' Visionary Leadership

Dive into the visionary leadership of Steve Jobs. Jobs' ability to envision transformative products and inspire his team reflects the Philippians mindset of pressing forward toward a higher calling in the pursuit of excellence.

2. Purposeful Innovation: Creating Impactful Solutions

Infuse purpose into innovation, creating solutions that not only meet market needs but also contribute to the greater good. Explore how purposeful innovation aligns with the Philippians approach, driving entrepreneurial success with a focus on positive impact.

Example: Elon Musk's Innovative Ventures

Learn from Elon Musk's ventures driven by purposeful innovation. Musk's commitment to solving global challenges through companies like Tesla and SpaceX illustrates the transformative power of aligning entrepreneurship with a higher purpose.

3. Resilience in Business: Turning Setbacks into Success

Forge resilience in the face of entrepreneurial challenges, viewing setbacks as opportunities for growth and refinement. Explore strategies for building resilience, allowing you to navigate the complexities of business with determination and adaptability.

Example: Oprah Winfrey's Business Resilience

Explore Oprah Winfrey's journey of resilience in the media industry. Oprah's ability to overcome challenges and build a successful media empire reflects the Philippians mindset of pressing on toward the goal, even in the face of adversity.

4. Customer-Centric Philanthropy: A Business Approach

Integrate customer-centric philanthropy into your business model, aligning profit with purpose. Explore how businesses can contribute to societal well-being, fostering a sustainable and impactful approach to entrepreneurship.

Example: TOMS' One for One Model

Dive into TOMS' One for One business model. TOMS' commitment to providing shoes for those in need for every pair sold exemplifies how customer-centric philanthropy aligns with the Philippians principle of pressing toward a higher calling.

5. Ethical Entrepreneurship: Building Trust and Integrity

Cultivate ethical entrepreneurship by prioritizing trust and integrity in your business practices. Explore how aligning your entrepreneurial pursuits with ethical principles contributes to long-term success and positive societal impact.

Example: Patagonia's Commitment to Ethical Practices

Learn from Patagonia's commitment to ethical and sustainable practices. Patagonia's focus on environmental stewardship and fair labor practices showcases how ethical entrepreneurship aligns with the Philippians principle of pursuing excellence with integrity.

Applying Philippians Principles to Entrepreneurial Mastery

Apply the principles derived from Philippians to your entrepreneurial journey, offering actionable insights for comprehensive business excellence.

1. Mission-Driven Business: Aligning Values with Ventures

Explore strategies for building a mission-driven business, aligning your entrepreneurial ventures with your values and goals. Learn how the

Philippians approach to purposeful focus contributes to the success of businesses driven by a higher calling.

2. Strategic Innovation: Navigating the Business Landscape

Delve into the principles of strategic innovation in entrepreneurship. Explore how a Philippians mindset guides strategic decision-making, fostering innovation that not only meets market demands but also contributes to societal progress.

3. Resilient Entrepreneurship: Overcoming Challenges with Determination

Understand how the principles of resilience apply to entrepreneurship. Explore strategies for navigating business challenges with determination, embracing setbacks as opportunities for learning and growth.

Your Entrepreneurial Mastery Toolkit: Practical Strategies for Daily Application

As you conclude this chapter, discover practical tools and exercises to integrate the Philippians approach to entrepreneurial excellence into your daily business endeavors. These tools will serve as your allies in cultivating an entrepreneurial mindset grounded in continuous growth, purposeful focus, and unwavering commitment.

Conclusion: The Philippians Entrepreneur's Legacy

Chapter Twelve sets the stage for an entrepreneurial legacy characterized by purposeful success—a journey where continuous growth, purposeful focus, and unwavering commitment converge to empower your pursuit of business excellence. As you embrace the teachings of Philippians 3:12-14, envision your entrepreneurial path as a testament to the transformative power of aligning your ventures with timeless principles, leaving an indelible mark on the business world through your positive contributions.

Chapter Thirteen: Overcoming Obstacles: A Philippians Perspective

———

Embark on a transformative journey of overcoming obstacles guided by the enduring wisdom of Philippians 3:12-14. In this chapter, explore the profound insights that empower individuals to face challenges with resilience, continuous growth, and unwavering determination. By embracing the Philippians perspective, discover how obstacles become steppingstones to personal and professional triumph.

Philippians 3:12-14: A Beacon in Times of Adversity

"Not that I have already obtained this or am already perfect, but I press on to make it my own because Christ Jesus has made me his own. Brothers, I do not consider that I have made it my own. But one thing I do: forgetting what lies behind and straining forward to what lies ahead, I press on toward the goal for the prize of the upward call of God in Christ Jesus." - Philippians 3:12-14 (ESV)

Allow these verses to illuminate your path through adversity, where continuous growth, purposeful focus, and unwavering commitment become powerful tools in overcoming life's challenges.

1. Resilience in the Face of Setbacks

Cultivate resilience as a foundational strength when confronted with obstacles. Explore how the Philippians mindset encourages individuals to view setbacks as opportunities for growth and development, fostering the resilience needed to navigate life's challenges.

Example: Nelson Mandela's Triumph Over Adversity

Dive into Nelson Mandela's journey of resilience during his imprisonment. Mandela's ability to emerge from incarceration with grace and forgiveness exemplifies the transformative power of resilience in overcoming profound obstacles.

2. Learning from Failure: A Philippians Approach

Embrace failure as a teacher on the path to success. Explore how the Philippians perspective encourages individuals to learn from mistakes, let go of past failures, and press forward with newfound wisdom and determination.

Example: Thomas Edison's Persistence

Discover the story of Thomas Edison's journey to invent the light bulb. Edison's numerous attempts and failures highlight the Philippians mindset of pressing on, ultimately leading to one of the most transformative inventions in history.

3. Adapting to Change: The Philippians Mindset

Navigate the ever-changing landscape of life with adaptability and flexibility. Explore how the Philippians approach encourages individuals to embrace change, view challenges as opportunities for growth, and adapt with resilience and determination.

Example: Jeff Bezos' Adaptability in Business

Learn from Jeff Bezos' transformative leadership at Amazon. Bezos' ability to adapt to the evolving e-commerce landscape reflects the Philippians mindset of pressing forward, embracing change, and turning challenges into opportunities.

4. Overcoming Fear and Doubt

Confront and overcome fear and doubt with a Philippians perspective. Explore how individuals can cultivate a mindset of faith and determination, enabling them to press forward with courage even in the face of uncertainty.

Example: J.K. Rowling's Battle with Self-Doubt

Dive into J.K. Rowling's personal struggles with self-doubt. Rowling's journey to overcome doubt and adversity in her writing career illustrates the transformative power of faith and perseverance in the face of obstacles.

5. Building Inner Strength: A Philippians Journey

Develop inner strength that serves as a reservoir of resilience. Explore how the Philippians perspective empowers individuals to build mental and emotional strength, allowing them to face challenges with fortitude and unwavering determination.

Example: Malala Yousafzai's Inner Strength

Explore Malala Yousafzai's unwavering commitment to education despite facing threats and violence. Malala's inner strength and determination showcase the transformative power of pressing forward in the face of adversity.

Applying Philippians Principles to Overcoming Obstacles

Apply the principles derived from Philippians to your journey of overcoming obstacles, offering actionable insights for cultivating resilience and triumph in the face of challenges.

1. Resilience Practices: Nurturing Inner Strength

Explore practical resilience practices that nurture inner strength. Learn how daily habits and mindset shifts inspired by Philippians principles can fortify your ability to overcome obstacles.

2. Learning from Setbacks: Turning Adversity into Wisdom

Delve into strategies for learning from setbacks and turning adversity into wisdom. Discover how the Philippians approach encourages a mindset of continuous growth and improvement, even in the midst of challenges.

3. Courage in the Face of Fear: A Philippians Mindset

Understand how the Philippians mindset cultivates courage in the face of fear. Explore practical steps for confronting and overcoming fear, allowing you to press forward with determination and faith.

Your Resilience Toolkit: Practical Strategies for Daily Application

As you conclude this chapter, discover practical tools and exercises to integrate the Philippians approach to overcoming obstacles into your daily life. These tools will serve as your allies in cultivating resilience, continuous growth, and unwavering determination, empowering you to triumph over life's challenges.

A Philippians Triumph Over Adversity

Chapter Thirteen sets the stage for a life characterized by triumph over adversity—a journey where continuous growth, purposeful focus, and unwavering commitment converge to empower your pursuit of success. As you embrace the teachings of Philippians 3:12-14, envision your path as a testament to the transformative power of aligning obstacles with timeless principles, leaving an indelible mark on the world through your resilience and triumph.

Chapter Fourteen: Balancing Work and Life with Intentionality

In the pursuit of holistic success and fulfillment, achieving a balance between work and personal life is paramount. Guided by the timeless wisdom of Philippians 3:12-14, this chapter explores the transformative power of intentional living. Learn to navigate the complexities of work and personal responsibilities with purposeful focus, continuous growth, and unwavering commitment to a harmonious life.

Philippians 3:12-14: A Call to Balance in Every Area

"I don't mean to say that I have already achieved these things or that I have already reached perfection. But I press on to possess that perfection for which Christ Jesus first possessed me. No, dear brothers and sisters, I have not achieved it, but I focus on this one thing: Forgetting the past and looking forward to what lies ahead, I press on to reach the end of the race and receive the heavenly prize for which God, through Christ Jesus, is calling us." - Philippians 3:12-14 (NLT)

Let these verses be your guide in harmonizing the various facets of life, where continuous growth, purposeful focus, and unwavering commitment converge to empower your pursuit of a balanced and fulfilling existence.

1. Work-Life Integration: A Philippians Approach

Embrace the concept of work-life integration guided by Philippians principles. Explore how intentional living allows you to seamlessly weave together your professional responsibilities and personal pursuits, creating a harmonious and fulfilling life.

Example: Sheryl Sandberg's Lean In Mentality

Dive into Sheryl Sandberg's advocacy for work-life integration. Sandberg's Lean In mentality emphasizes the importance of women leaning into their professional roles while maintaining a balanced and intentional approach to life.

2. Setting Priorities with Purposeful Focus

Cultivate purposeful focus in setting priorities for both work and personal life. Explore strategies for aligning your daily tasks with your long-term goals, ensuring that your efforts contribute to a well-rounded and meaningful existence.

Example: Warren Buffett's Priority Pyramid

Learn from Warren Buffett's approach to setting priorities. Buffett's Priority Pyramid emphasizes focusing on the essential and saying no to non-essential tasks, showcasing how intentional prioritization leads to a more balanced life.

3. Mindful Time Management

Practice mindful time management to optimize productivity and well-being. Explore techniques for balancing work commitments and personal time, allowing you to make the most of each moment with intentionality and purpose.

Example: Bill Gates' Time-Blocking Strategy

Discover Bill Gates' time-blocking strategy. Gates allocates specific blocks of time for different activities, emphasizing the importance of intentional time management in achieving a harmonious balance between work and personal life.

4. Nurturing Relationships: A Philippians Perspective

Understand the importance of nurturing relationships in both work and personal spheres. Explore how the Philippians perspective encourages individuals to build meaningful connections, fostering a support system that contributes to overall well-being.

Example: Richard Branson's Emphasis on Work-Life Blend

Delve into Richard Branson's philosophy of work-life blend. Branson emphasizes the interconnectedness of work and personal life, showcasing how nurturing relationships in both realms contributes to a more fulfilling existence.

5. Rest and Renewal: The Philippians Sabbath

Recognize the significance of rest and renewal in maintaining a balanced life. Explore how the Philippians principle of pressing forward is complemented by intentional periods of rest, allowing for rejuvenation and sustained excellence.

Example: Jeff Weiner's Embrace of Mindfulness

Learn from Jeff Weiner's embrace of mindfulness and intentional breaks. Weiner emphasizes the importance of incorporating moments of rest and renewal into the workday, promoting a healthier and more balanced lifestyle.

Applying Philippians Principles to Balanced Living

Apply the principles derived from Philippians to your journey of balancing work and life, offering actionable insights for a harmonious and intentional existence.

1. Reflective Practices: Evaluating Life Alignment

Explore reflective practices to evaluate the alignment of your life with your values and goals. Learn how the Philippians approach encourages introspection and intentional adjustments to create a more balanced existence.

2. Goal Setting for Harmony: Aligning Ambitions

Delve into goal-setting practices that align your professional ambitions with personal fulfillment. Discover how the Philippians mindset contributes to setting intentional goals that lead to a harmonious and purpose-driven life.

3. Sabbath Living: Intentional Rest and Rejuvenation

Understand the concept of Sabbath living in the Philippians context. Explore intentional practices for rest and rejuvenation, fostering a lifestyle that combines productivity with periods of renewal for sustained well-being.

Your Balanced Living Toolkit: Practical Strategies for Daily Application

As you conclude this chapter, discover practical tools and exercises to integrate the Philippians approach to balanced living into your daily life. These tools will serve as your allies in cultivating intentional living, continuous growth, and unwavering commitment, empowering you to harmonize the various aspects of your life.

The Philippians Symphony of Life

Chapter Fourteen sets the stage for a symphony of life characterized by intentional harmony—a journey where continuous growth, purposeful focus, and unwavering commitment converge to empower your pursuit of a balanced and fulfilling existence. As you embrace the teachings of Philippians 3:12-14, envision your life as a testament to the transformative power of aligning work and personal pursuits with timeless principles, leaving an indelible mark on the world through your intentional and harmonious living.

Chapter Fifteen: Leadership Lessons from Philippians

Embark on a transformative exploration of leadership principles grounded in the timeless wisdom of Philippians 3:12-14. In this chapter, uncover profound insights that transcend traditional leadership paradigms, fostering a style of leadership characterized by continuous growth, purposeful focus, and unwavering commitment. Learn to inspire and guide others with the spirit of Philippians, leaving an indelible mark on your leadership journey.

Philippians 3:12-14: A Call to Leadership Excellence

"I don't mean to say that I have already achieved these things or that I have already reached perfection. But I press on to possess that perfection for which Christ Jesus first possessed me. No, dear brothers and sisters, I have not achieved it, but I focus on this one thing: Forgetting the past and looking forward to what lies ahead, I press on to reach the end of the race and receive the heavenly prize for which God, through Christ Jesus, is calling us." - Philippians 3:12-14 (NLT)

Let these verses guide your leadership journey, where continuous growth, purposeful focus, and unwavering commitment converge to empower your pursuit of leadership excellence.

1. Visionary Leadership: Forward-Looking Focus

Embrace visionary leadership with a forward-looking focus inspired by Philippians. Explore how aligning your leadership vision with a higher purpose allows you to inspire and guide your team toward shared goals and aspirations.

Example: Martin Luther King Jr.'s Dream for Equality

Dive into Martin Luther King Jr.'s visionary leadership for civil rights. King's dream of equality and justice reflects the Philippians mindset of pressing forward toward a higher calling, inspiring others to join in the pursuit of a better future.

2. Servant Leadership: A Philippians Humility

Cultivate servant leadership anchored in Philippians humility. Explore how adopting a mindset of serving others fosters trust, collaboration, and collective success within your team and organization.

Example: Mother Teresa's Humble Service

Learn from Mother Teresa's life of humble service. Mother Teresa's commitment to serving the impoverished reflects the Philippians principle of considering others as more significant than oneself, providing a powerful model for servant leadership.

3. Resilient Leadership: Overcoming Challenges with Determination

Forge resilient leadership in the face of challenges, drawing strength from Philippians principles. Explore strategies for navigating obstacles with determination, resilience, and a commitment to continuous growth.

Example: Winston Churchill's Resilience in War

Delve into Winston Churchill's resilient leadership during World War II. Churchill's steadfast determination and resilience, even in the darkest times, exemplify the Philippians mindset of pressing on toward a higher goal for the greater good.

4. Inspirational Leadership: Igniting the Passion Within

Ignite passion within your team through inspirational leadership rooted in Philippians principles. Explore how fostering a sense of purpose, enthusiasm, and dedication leads to a motivated and high-performing team.

Example: Steve Jobs' Passion for Innovation

Explore Steve Jobs' inspirational leadership in the world of technology. Jobs' passion for innovation and his ability to inspire others to think differently exemplify the Philippians approach of pressing on toward transformative goals.

5. Adaptive Leadership: Embracing Change with Purpose

Embrace adaptive leadership with purpose, aligning with the Philippians mindset of pressing forward in the face of change. Explore how leaders can navigate and lead their teams through evolving landscapes with flexibility and resilience.

Example: Satya Nadella's Transformation at Microsoft

Learn from Satya Nadella's adaptive leadership at Microsoft. Nadella's ability to lead the company through a transformative journey reflects the Philippians principle of embracing change with a purposeful focus on the future.

Applying Philippians Principles to Leadership Mastery

Apply the principles derived from Philippians to your leadership journey, offering actionable insights for comprehensive leadership excellence.

1. Vision Casting: Communicating a Forward Focus

Explore strategies for effective vision casting as a leader. Learn how to communicate a forward-looking focus inspired by Philippians, inspiring your team to press on toward shared goals and aspirations.

2. Humility in Leadership: Servant Leadership Practices

Delve into servant leadership practices that cultivate humility. Understand how leading with humility, considering the needs of others, and fostering a collaborative environment contribute to successful leadership.

3. Resilient Leadership Habits: Navigating Challenges

Understand habits that foster resilient leadership. Explore practical ways to navigate challenges with determination, drawing strength from the Philippians mindset of pressing on toward a higher goal.

Your Leadership Mastery Toolkit: Practical Strategies for Daily Application

As you conclude this chapter, discover practical tools and exercises to integrate the Philippians approach to leadership excellence into your daily leadership practices. These tools will serve as your allies in cultivating visionary, servant, resilient, inspirational, and adaptive leadership—empowering you to make a lasting impact on your team and organization.

The Philippians Leader's Legacy

Chapter Fifteen sets the stage for a leadership legacy characterized by excellence—a journey where continuous growth, purposeful focus, and unwavering commitment converge to empower your pursuit of leadership greatness. As you embrace the teachings of Philippians 3:12-14, envision your leadership path as a testament to the transformative power of aligning your leadership style with timeless principles, leaving an indelible mark on the world through your visionary, servant-hearted, and resilient leadership.

Chapter Sixteen: Mindfulness in the Digital Age

In the bustling landscape of the digital age, cultivating mindfulness becomes essential for a balanced and purposeful life. Guided by the timeless wisdom of Philippians 3:12-14, this chapter explores the transformative power of mindfulness, offering insights and practical strategies to navigate the digital world with continuous growth, purposeful focus, and unwavering commitment.

Philippians 3:12-14: A Blueprint for Mindful Living

"I don't mean to say that I have already achieved these things or that I have already reached perfection. But I press on to possess that perfection for which Christ Jesus first possessed me. No, dear brothers and sisters, I have not achieved it, but I focus on this one thing: Forgetting the past and looking forward to what lies ahead, I press on to reach the end of the race and receive the heavenly prize for which God, through Christ Jesus, is calling us." - Philippians 3:12-14 (NLT)

Let these verses guide your journey to mindful living in the digital age, where continuous growth, purposeful focus, and unwavering commitment converge to empower your pursuit of a balanced and intentional existence.

1. Digital Detox: A Philippians Retreat

Explore the concept of a digital detox as a form of pressing forward. Learn how intentionally disconnecting from digital distractions allows for mental and emotional rejuvenation, fostering mindfulness and clarity.

Example: Bill Gates' Think Week

Dive into Bill Gates' Think Week, a period during which he disconnects from the digital world to read and reflect. Gates' practice exemplifies the Philippians mindset of intentionally pressing forward by taking breaks for focused contemplation.

2. Mindful Consumption: Nourishing Your Mind

Cultivate mindful consumption habits in the digital realm. Explore how being intentional about the content you engage with online contributes to a healthier and more purposeful digital experience.

Example: Warren Buffett's Information Diet

Learn from Warren Buffett's information diet, where he focuses on quality over quantity when consuming news. Buffett's approach aligns with the Philippians principle of intentional focus on what truly matters.

3. Digital Boundaries: Fostering Balance

Establish digital boundaries to foster a balanced life. Explore strategies for setting limits on screen time, notifications, and online activities to ensure a mindful approach to technology usage.

Example: Mark Zuckerberg's Tech Limits for Family

Discover Mark Zuckerberg's practice of setting tech limits for his family. Zuckerberg's approach reflects the Philippians mindset of intentional focus on family and personal life, demonstrating the importance of digital boundaries.

4. Mindful Communication: Building Meaningful Connections

Practice mindful communication in the digital age. Explore how intentional and meaningful interactions online contribute to building genuine connections and fostering a positive digital environment.

Example: Elon Musk's Thoughtful Social Media Engagement

Dive into Elon Musk's approach to social media engagement. Musk's thoughtful and intentional communication style aligns with the Philippians principle of considering the impact of words on others.

5. Digital Mindfulness Practices: Integration into Daily Life

Integrate digital mindfulness practices into your daily life. Explore practical techniques, such as meditation apps, mindful breathing exercises, and digital well-being tools, to promote mindfulness in the midst of the digital hustle.

Example: Oprah Winfrey's Mindful Moments

Learn from Oprah Winfrey's commitment to mindful moments throughout the day. Winfrey's practice exemplifies the Philippians mindset of intentionally taking moments of pause and reflection amid a busy schedule.

Applying Philippians Principles to Digital Mindfulness

Apply the principles derived from Philippians to your journey of digital mindfulness, offering actionable insights for navigating the digital age with continuous growth, purposeful focus, and unwavering commitment.

1. Mindful Tech Habits: Balancing Digital Engagement

Explore strategies for cultivating mindful tech habits. Learn how the Philippians approach guides intentional choices in digital engagement, ensuring that technology enhances rather than detracts from your overall well-being.

2. Purposeful Digital Engagement: Aligning with Values

Delve into purposeful digital engagement aligned with your values. Discover how the Philippians mindset encourages you to be intentional about the content you create and consume, ensuring that it aligns with your overarching goals.

3. Mindful Tech Breaks: Nurturing Mental Wellness

Understand the importance of mindful tech breaks for nurturing mental wellness. Explore how intentional breaks from digital devices contribute to mental clarity and focus, aligning with the Philippians principle of pressing forward with purpose.

Your Digital Mindfulness Toolkit: Practical Strategies for Daily Application

As you conclude this chapter, discover practical tools and exercises to integrate the Philippians approach to digital mindfulness into your daily life. These tools will serve as your allies in cultivating continuous growth, purposeful focus, and unwavering commitment in the midst of the digital age.

The Philippians Digital Pilgrimage

Chapter Sixteen sets the stage for a digital pilgrimage characterized by mindful living—a journey where continuous growth, purposeful focus, and unwavering commitment converge to empower your pursuit of a balanced and intentional existence in the digital age. As you embrace the teachings of Philippians 3:12-14, envision your digital path as a testament to the transformative power of aligning technology usage with timeless principles, leaving an indelible mark on the world through your mindful and purposeful engagement in the digital realm.

Chapter Seventeen: Nurturing a Positive Mindset

Discover the transformative power of cultivating a positive mindset, guided by the timeless wisdom of Philippians 3:12-14. In this chapter, explore actionable insights and practical strategies to foster a positive outlook on life, enabling you to navigate challenges with continuous growth, purposeful focus, and unwavering commitment.

Philippians 3:12-14: A Beacon of Positivity

"I don't mean to say that I have already achieved these things or that I have already reached perfection. But I press on to possess that perfection for which Christ Jesus first possessed me. No, dear brothers and sisters, I have not achieved it, but I focus on this one thing: Forgetting the past and looking forward to what lies ahead, I press on to reach the end of the race and receive the heavenly prize for which God, through Christ Jesus, is calling us." - Philippians 3:12-14 (NLT)

Let these verses illuminate your path to cultivating a positive mindset, where continuous growth, purposeful focus, and unwavering commitment converge to empower your pursuit of a more optimistic and fulfilling life.

1. Gratitude Practices: Cultivating Thankfulness

Cultivate gratitude as a cornerstone of a positive mindset. Explore practical gratitude practices that shift your focus towards the positive aspects of life, fostering a sense of appreciation and contentment.

Example: Oprah Winfrey's Gratitude Journaling

Dive into Oprah Winfrey's practice of daily gratitude journaling. Winfrey's commitment to acknowledging and appreciating the positive aspects of each day reflects the Philippians mindset of focusing on the good and pressing forward.

2. Positive Affirmations: Shaping Thought Patterns

Harness the power of positive affirmations to shape your thought patterns. Explore how intentional and uplifting self-talk can contribute to a positive mindset, aligning with the Philippians principle of pressing forward with affirmations of hope and faith.

Example: Muhammad Ali's Affirmations of Greatness

Discover Muhammad Ali's iconic affirmations of greatness. Ali's intentional use of positive affirmations exemplifies the Philippians mindset of speaking positive truths over one's life, fostering a mindset of success and resilience.

3. Resilience Through Challenges: A Philippians Approach

Navigate challenges with resilience and a positive perspective. Explore how the Philippians approach encourages individuals to view obstacles as opportunities for growth, fostering a mindset of resilience and determination.

Example: Malala Yousafzai's Resilience in Adversity

Delve into Malala Yousafzai's resilience in the face of adversity. Malala's positive mindset and commitment to education, despite facing threats, align with the Philippians principle of pressing forward with purpose in the midst of challenges.

4. Positive Visualization: Envisioning Success

Practice positive visualization to envision success and abundance. Explore how creating vivid mental images of your desired outcomes aligns with the Philippians mindset of pressing forward toward the heavenly prize.

Example: Jim Carrey's Visualization for Success

Learn from Jim Carrey's use of positive visualization for success. Carrey's story of writing himself a check for future success showcases the transformative power of envisioning positive outcomes aligned with the Philippians principle.

5. Positivity in Relationships: Nurturing Connections

Foster positivity in relationships by cultivating kindness and encouragement. Explore how intentional and positive interactions contribute to meaningful connections, aligning with the Philippians principle of considering others as more significant than oneself.

Example: Fred Rogers' Positive Influence

Discover Fred Rogers' positive influence in the realm of children's television. Mr. Rogers' commitment to kindness and positivity exemplifies the Philippians mindset of considering others with love and compassion.

Applying Philippians Principles to Positive Living

Apply the principles derived from Philippians to your journey of nurturing a positive mindset, offering actionable insights for infusing optimism into your daily life.

1. Daily Positive Habits: Creating a Joyful Routine

Explore daily positive habits that contribute to a joyful routine. Learn how the Philippians approach encourages intentional practices that bring joy and positivity into your everyday life.

2. Affirmation Rituals: Speaking Life Daily

Delve into affirmation rituals for speaking life daily. Discover how the Philippians mindset inspires the intentional use of affirmations to shape thoughts and foster positivity.

3. Resilient Thought Patterns: Facing Challenges with Faith

Understand how resilient thought patterns can be cultivated through faith. Explore the Philippians perspective of facing challenges with unwavering faith and a positive mindset.

Your Positive Living Toolkit: Practical Strategies for Daily Application

As you conclude this chapter, discover practical tools and exercises to integrate the Philippians approach to positive living into your daily routine. These tools will serve as your allies in cultivating continuous growth, purposeful focus, and unwavering commitment in the pursuit of a positive and fulfilling life.

The Philippians Path to Positivity

Chapter Seventeen sets the stage for a positive journey characterized by continuous growth—a life where purposeful focus and unwavering commitment converge to empower your pursuit of a more optimistic and fulfilling existence. As you embrace the teachings of Philippians 3:12-14, envision your path as a testament to the transformative power of aligning your mindset with timeless principles, leaving an indelible mark on the world through your positive outlook and resilience.

Chapter Eighteen: Philippians and the Art of Effective Communication

———

Embark on a journey into the transformative realm of effective communication, guided by the timeless wisdom of Philippians 3:12-14. In this chapter, explore actionable insights and practical strategies to enhance your communication skills, enabling you to connect more deeply with others and navigate life's challenges with continuous growth, purposeful focus, and unwavering commitment.

Philippians 3:12-14: A Foundation for Effective Connection

"I don't mean to say that I have already achieved these things or that I have already reached perfection. But I press on to possess that perfection for which Christ Jesus first possessed me. No, dear brothers and sisters, I have not achieved it, but I focus on this one thing: Forgetting the past and looking forward to what lies ahead, I press on to reach the end of the race and receive the heavenly prize for which God, through Christ Jesus, is calling us." - Philippians 3:12-14 (NLT)

Let these verses illuminate your path to effective communication, where continuous growth, purposeful focus, and unwavering commitment converge to empower your pursuit of meaningful connections and impactful conversations.

1. The Power of Listening: A Philippians Humility

Discover the transformative power of active listening. Explore how adopting a Philippians mindset of humility allows you to genuinely hear and understand others, fostering deeper connections and more meaningful communication.

Example: Maya Angelou's Empathetic Listening

Dive into Maya Angelou's legacy of empathetic listening. Angelou's ability to connect with people through genuine listening reflects the Philippians principle of considering others as more significant than oneself.

2. Clear and Concise Expression: Philippians Precision

Master the art of clear and concise expression inspired by the precision of Philippians. Explore how communicating with purpose and clarity aligns with the Philippians mindset of pressing forward with a focused message.

Example: Martin Luther King Jr.'s I Have a Dream Speech

Delve into Martin Luther King Jr.'s iconic "I Have a Dream" speech. King's ability to convey a powerful message with clarity and precision mirrors the Philippians approach of focused communication for impactful change.

3. Empathetic Communication: A Philippians Compassion

Cultivate empathetic communication grounded in Philippians compassion. Explore how understanding and sharing in the feelings of others fosters genuine connections, aligning with the Philippians principle of considering the needs of others.

Example: Brené Brown's Vulnerability

Learn from Brené Brown's emphasis on vulnerability in communication. Brown's approach reflects the Philippians mindset of compassionate communication, allowing for authentic and meaningful connections.

4. Constructive Feedback: Philippians Edification

Offer and receive constructive feedback with a Philippians spirit of edification. Explore how providing feedback that builds and encourages aligns with the Philippians principle of pressing forward toward positive growth.

Example: Elon Musk's Feedback Culture

Delve into Elon Musk's leadership approach to constructive feedback. Musk's commitment to a culture of open communication and improvement resonates with the Philippians perspective of edifying one another.

5. Mindful Communication: Philippians Awareness

Practice mindful communication anchored in Philippians awareness. Explore how being present and intentional in your interactions fosters deeper connections and more impactful conversations.

Example: Thich Nhat Hanh's Mindful Communication Practices

Discover Thich Nhat Hanh's teachings on mindful communication. Nhat Hanh's practices align with the Philippians approach, emphasizing the importance of awareness and intentionality in communication.

Applying Philippians Principles to Effective Communication

Apply the principles derived from Philippians to your journey of effective communication, offering actionable insights for building meaningful connections and fostering impactful conversations.

1. Philippians Precision in Everyday Conversations

Explore how to incorporate Philippians precision into your everyday conversations. Learn to communicate with clarity and purpose, ensuring your message is focused and impactful.

2. Compassionate Communication Habits

Cultivate habits of compassionate communication in your interactions. Discover how considering the needs and feelings of others enhances the quality of your relationships, aligning with the Philippians mindset.

3. Edifying Feedback Practices

Incorporate edifying feedback practices into your personal and professional relationships. Learn how to provide constructive feedback that uplifts and encourages, contributing to continuous growth.

Your Effective Communication Toolkit: Practical Strategies for Daily Application

As you conclude this chapter, discover practical tools and exercises to integrate the Philippians approach to effective communication into your daily life. These tools will serve as your allies in cultivating continuous growth, purposeful focus, and unwavering commitment in your quest for meaningful connections and impactful conversations.

The Philippians Symphony of Connection

Chapter Eighteen sets the stage for a symphony of connection characterized by effective communication—a journey where continuous growth, purposeful focus, and unwavering commitment converge to empower your pursuit of meaningful and impactful conversations. As you embrace the teachings of Philippians 3:12-14, envision your communication style as a testament to the transformative power of aligning your words with timeless principles, leaving an indelible mark on the world through your ability to connect, understand, and uplift others.

Chapter Nineteen: Philippians and the Art of Effective Communication - Part Two

Embark on a continued exploration of the transformative realm of effective communication, guided by the timeless wisdom of Philippians 3:12-14. In this chapter, delve deeper into actionable insights and practical strategies, empowering you to refine your communication skills for even more profound connections and impactful conversations.

Philippians 3:12-14: Anchoring Communication Mastery

"I don't mean to say that I have already achieved these things or that I have already reached perfection. But I press on to possess that perfection for which Christ Jesus first possessed me. No, dear brothers and sisters, I have not achieved it, but I focus on this one thing: Forgetting the past and looking forward to what lies ahead, I press on to reach the end of the race and receive the heavenly prize for which God, through Christ Jesus, is calling us." - Philippians 3:12-14 (NLT)

Let these verses be the anchor for your journey to communication mastery, where continuous growth, purposeful focus, and unwavering commitment converge to empower your pursuit of even more meaningful connections and impactful conversations.

1. Authenticity in Communication: A Philippians Transparency

Embrace authenticity as a cornerstone of effective communication. Explore how transparency and genuine self-expression align with the Philippians mindset of pressing forward with honesty and authenticity.

Example: Michelle Obama's Authentic Storytelling

Dive into Michelle Obama's approach to authentic storytelling. Obama's ability to connect through sharing her personal journey exemplifies the Philippians principle of transparent communication, fostering genuine connections.

2. Emotional Intelligence: Philippians Sensitivity

Cultivate emotional intelligence in your communication. Explore how understanding and navigating emotions, both yours and others', align with the Philippians mindset of considering the needs and feelings of others.

Example: Daniel Goleman's Leadership through Emotional Intelligence

Learn from Daniel Goleman's insights on leadership through emotional intelligence. Goleman's teachings align with the Philippians approach, emphasizing the importance of empathy and sensitivity in effective communication.

3. Nonverbal Communication Mastery: A Philippians Presence

Master the art of nonverbal communication, embodying a Philippians presence. Explore how body language, facial expressions, and gestures contribute to the effectiveness of your message, aligning with the Philippians principle of intentional communication.

Example: Oprah Winfrey's Nonverbal Impact

Delve into Oprah Winfrey's nonverbal impact in her communication. Winfrey's ability to convey empathy and connection through nonverbal cues aligns with the Philippians mindset of intentional and impactful communication.

4. Conflict Resolution: Philippians Reconciliation

Navigate conflicts with a Philippians spirit of reconciliation. Explore strategies for resolving disagreements with empathy and understanding, aligning with the Philippians principle of considering others as more significant than oneself.

Example: Nelson Mandela's Approach to Reconciliation

Learn from Nelson Mandela's approach to reconciliation in post-apartheid South Africa. Mandela's commitment to understanding and forgiveness exemplifies the Philippians mindset of seeking unity and resolution in communication.

5. The Art of Persuasion: Philippians Influence

Hone the art of persuasion, aligning with the Philippians influence. Explore how communicating with conviction, empathy, and a focus on the greater good aligns with the Philippians principle of pressing forward toward a higher goal.

Example: Steve Jobs' Persuasive Presentations

Dive into Steve Jobs' persuasive presentation style. Jobs' ability to inspire and influence through compelling communication reflects the Philippians mindset of pressing on toward transformative goals for the greater good.

Applying Philippians Principles to Advanced Communication Mastery

Apply the principles derived from Philippians to elevate your communication mastery, offering advanced insights for building even more meaningful connections and fostering impactful conversations.

1. Mastering the Art of Transparent Communication

Explore advanced strategies for mastering transparent communication. Learn to navigate vulnerability, share your authentic story, and build deeper connections with those around you.

2. Cultivating High-Level Emotional Intelligence

Delve into high-level emotional intelligence practices. Enhance your ability to understand and navigate complex emotions in yourself and others, fostering deeper empathy and connection.

3. Elevating Nonverbal Communication Proficiency

Enhance your proficiency in nonverbal communication. Fine-tune your body language, facial expressions, and gestures to convey intention and impact, aligning with the Philippians principle of intentional communication.

Your Advanced Communication Mastery Toolkit: Practical Strategies for Daily Application

As you conclude this chapter, discover practical tools and exercises to integrate the Philippians approach to advanced communication mastery into your daily life. These tools will serve as your allies in cultivating continuous growth, purposeful focus, and unwavering commitment as you elevate your communication skills to new heights.

The Philippians Symphony of Impactful Communication

Chapter Nineteen sets the stage for a symphony of impactful communication characterized by advanced mastery—a journey where continuous growth, purposeful focus, and unwavering commitment converge to empower your pursuit of even more meaningful connections and influential conversations. As you embrace the teachings of Philippians 3:12-14, envision your communication style as a testament to the transformative power.

Chapter Twenty: Legacy Building - Leaving a Lasting Impact

Embark on a profound exploration of legacy building, guided by the timeless wisdom of Philippians 3:12-14. In this chapter, discover actionable insights and practical strategies to shape your legacy, enabling you to leave a lasting impact on the world with continuous growth, purposeful focus, and unwavering commitment.

Philippians 3:12-14: A Blueprint for Legacy Building

"I don't mean to say that I have already achieved these things or that I have already reached perfection. But I press on to possess that perfection for which Christ Jesus first possessed me. No, dear brothers and sisters, I have not achieved it, but I focus on this one thing: Forgetting the past and looking forward to what lies ahead, I press on to reach the end of the race and receive the heavenly prize for which God, through Christ Jesus, is calling us." - Philippians 3:12-14 (NLT)

Let these verses guide your journey to legacy building, where continuous growth, purposeful focus, and unwavering commitment converge to empower your pursuit of leaving a meaningful and lasting impact on the world.

1. Purpose-Driven Living: A Philippians Calling

Embrace purpose-driven living as the cornerstone of legacy building. Explore how aligning your actions with a higher calling, as outlined in Philippians, creates a foundation for leaving a lasting impact on others and the world.

Example: Mother Teresa's Purpose-Driven Service

Dive into Mother Teresa's life of purpose-driven service. Her unwavering commitment to serving the poor and vulnerable reflects the Philippians principle of pressing forward toward a heavenly calling, leaving an indelible legacy of compassion.

2. Impactful Contributions: Philippians Excellence

Make impactful contributions to the world by pursuing excellence in your endeavors. Explore how the Philippians pursuit of perfection aligns with the commitment to leave a legacy marked by the highest standards of achievement.

Example: Leonardo da Vinci's Pursuit of Excellence

Delve into Leonardo da Vinci's pursuit of excellence in art and innovation. Da Vinci's commitment to pushing the boundaries of knowledge and creativity embodies the Philippians mindset of pressing on toward perfection, leaving an enduring legacy of genius.

3. Mentoring and Empowering Others: Philippians Mentorship

Invest in mentoring and empowering others as a key element of legacy building. Explore how the Philippians principle of considering others as more significant than oneself manifests in guiding and uplifting the next generation.

Example: Maya Angelou's Legacy of Mentorship

Learn from Maya Angelou's legacy of mentorship and empowerment. Angelou's commitment to nurturing and guiding aspiring writers reflects the Philippians principle of selfless mentorship, leaving a lasting impact on literature and humanity.

4. Philanthropy and Social Impact: A Philippians Compassion

Engage in philanthropy and social impact with a Philippians spirit of compassion. Explore how contributing to the well-being of others aligns with the Philippians mindset of considering the needs of the community, leaving a legacy of positive change.

Example: Bill and Melinda Gates Foundation's Global Impact

Dive into the global impact of the Bill and Melinda Gates Foundation. Their dedication to addressing global health and poverty issues mirrors the Philippians principle of considering others and leaving a lasting legacy of transformative change.

5. Transcending Challenges: Philippians Resilience

Transcend challenges with Philippians resilience as a defining trait of your legacy. Explore how facing adversity with faith and perseverance aligns with the Philippians mindset of pressing forward, leaving a legacy marked by strength and resilience.

Example: Nelson Mandela's Legacy of Forgiveness

Explore Nelson Mandela's legacy of forgiveness and reconciliation. Mandela's ability to overcome personal and societal challenges reflects the Philippians principle of pressing on through difficulties, leaving a legacy of peace and unity.

Applying Philippians Principles to Legacy Building Mastery

Apply the principles derived from Philippians to master the art of legacy building, offering actionable insights for leaving an enduring impact on the world.

1. Intentional Living for Legacy

Live intentionally with your legacy in mind. Explore strategies for aligning your daily choices and actions with the enduring impact you wish to leave on the world.

2. Continuous Growth for Timeless Impact

Embrace continuous growth for timeless impact. Learn how the pursuit of personal and professional development aligns with the Philippians mindset of pressing on toward perfection, leaving a legacy marked by growth.

3. Cultivating a Philippians Mindset in Leadership

Cultivate a Philippians mindset in leadership. Explore how leading with humility, compassion, and a commitment to others fosters a legacy of positive influence and lasting impact.

Your Legacy Building Mastery Toolkit: Practical Strategies for Daily Application

As you conclude this chapter, discover practical tools and exercises to integrate the Philippians approach to legacy building.

Chapter Twenty-One: Innovation through Focused Creativity

Embark on a journey into the realm of innovation, guided by the timeless wisdom of Philippians 3:12-14. In this chapter, explore the intersection of focused creativity and continuous growth, purposeful focus, and unwavering commitment, unlocking the key to groundbreaking innovations that leave a lasting impact.

Philippians 3:12-14: Inspiring Innovative Paths

"I don't mean to say that I have already achieved these things or that I have already reached perfection. But I press on to possess that perfection for which Christ Jesus first possessed me. No, dear brothers and sisters, I have not achieved it, but I focus on this one thing: Forgetting the past and looking forward to what lies ahead, I press on to reach the end of the race and receive the heavenly prize for which God, through Christ Jesus, is calling us." - Philippians 3:12-14 (NLT)

Let these verses be the guiding force for unleashing innovative potential, where continuous growth, purposeful focus, and unwavering commitment converge to inspire groundbreaking creativity.

1. Creativity Grounded in Purpose: A Philippians Vision

Discover the transformative power of creativity grounded in purpose. Explore how aligning your creative endeavors with a higher vision, as outlined in Philippians, becomes a catalyst for groundbreaking innovations that shape the future.

Example: Steve Jobs and Apple's Visionary Products

Dive into Steve Jobs' visionary approach at Apple. Jobs' commitment to merging technology with humanity's needs exemplifies the Philippians principle of pressing forward toward a heavenly vision, leaving an indelible legacy of innovative products.

2. Continuous Learning and Adaptation: Philippians Curiosity

Cultivate a culture of continuous learning and adaptation as the bedrock of innovation. Explore how the Philippians mindset of continuous growth aligns with the curiosity and adaptability required for groundbreaking creative solutions.

Example: Elon Musk's Multidisciplinary Approach

Delve into Elon Musk's multidisciplinary approach to innovation. Musk's commitment to learning across various fields mirrors the Philippians principle of pressing on toward perfection, resulting in groundbreaking advancements.

3. Collaborative Innovation: Philippians Unity

Foster collaborative innovation through a Philippians spirit of unity. Explore how working together, considering others' perspectives, and focusing on shared goals lead to groundbreaking solutions that impact communities and industries.

Example: Pixar's Collaborative Animation Process

Explore Pixar's collaborative animation process. The studio's commitment to a collaborative, unified approach aligns with the Philippians principle of considering others as more significant than oneself, resulting in groundbreaking animated films.

4. Embracing Failure as Growth: Philippians Resilience

Embrace failure as a pathway to growth and innovation. Explore how facing setbacks with resilience and a commitment to pressing forward aligns with the Philippians mindset, leading to groundbreaking creative breakthroughs.

Example: Thomas Edison's Perseverance with the Light Bulb

Delve into Thomas Edison's perseverance in inventing the light bulb. Edison's commitment to overcoming failures and setbacks aligns with the Philippians principle of pressing on through challenges, resulting in groundbreaking innovation.

5. Ethical Innovation: Philippians Integrity

Innovate with integrity, guided by ethical considerations. Explore how the Philippians mindset of considering the needs of others aligns with the responsibility to create groundbreaking solutions that positively impact society.

Example: Google's Ethical Approach to AI

Explore Google's ethical approach to artificial intelligence. The company's commitment to responsible and ethical innovation reflects the Philippians principle of considering others and leaving a positive legacy through groundbreaking advancements.

Applying Philippians Principles to Innovative Mastery

Apply the principles derived from Philippians to master the art of innovative thinking, offering actionable insights for fostering groundbreaking creativity and leaving a lasting impact.

1. Purpose-Driven Ideation

Infuse purpose into your ideation process. Explore how aligning your creative thoughts with a higher vision leads to groundbreaking ideas that contribute to positive change.

2. Curiosity as a Catalyst for Innovation

Cultivate curiosity as a catalyst for innovation. Learn how embracing a Philippians mindset of continuous growth fuels curiosity, propelling you toward groundbreaking solutions.

3. Fostering Collaborative Creativity

Foster collaborative creativity in your endeavors. Discover strategies for working collaboratively, considering diverse perspectives, and focusing on shared goals to achieve groundbreaking results.

Your Innovative Mastery Toolkit: Practical Strategies for Daily Application

As you conclude this chapter, discover practical tools and exercises to integrate the Philippians approach to innovative mastery into your daily life. These tools will serve as your allies in cultivating continuous growth, purposeful focus, and unwavering commitment as you unleash groundbreaking creativity and leave a lasting impact on the world.

Chapter Twenty-Two: Resolving Conflicts Philippians-Style

Embark on a transformative journey into conflict resolution, guided by the enduring wisdom of Philippians 3:12-14. In this chapter, discover the profound impact of resolving conflicts with continuous growth, purposeful focus, and unwavering commitment, creating a roadmap for harmonious relationships and lasting peace.

Philippians 3:12-14: A Blueprint for Conflict Resolution

"I don't mean to say that I have already achieved these things or that I have already reached perfection. But I press on to possess that perfection for which Christ Jesus first possessed me. No, dear brothers and sisters, I have not achieved it, but I focus on this one thing: Forgetting the past and looking forward to what lies ahead, I press on to reach the end of the race and receive the heavenly prize for which God, through Christ Jesus, is calling us." - Philippians 3:12-14 (NLT)

Let these verses be the guiding light for conflict resolution, where continuous growth, purposeful focus, and unwavering commitment converge to foster understanding, reconciliation, and peace.

1. Humility in Conflict: A Philippians Virtue

Cultivate humility as a virtuous approach to conflict resolution. Explore how adopting a humble attitude, considering others' perspectives, aligns with the Philippians mindset of considering others as more significant than oneself.

Example: Mahatma Gandhi's Humble Leadership

Delve into Mahatma Gandhi's humble approach to leadership and conflict resolution. Gandhi's commitment to humility and understanding exemplifies the Philippians principle of pressing forward in conflicts with a spirit of humility.

2. Active Listening and Empathy: Philippians Understanding

Practice active listening and empathy as foundational elements in conflict resolution. Explore how truly understanding others' feelings and perspectives aligns with the Philippians principle of considering the needs and feelings of others.

Example: Nelson Mandela's Empathetic Leadership

Learn from Nelson Mandela's empathetic leadership in South Africa's reconciliation process. Mandela's ability to listen actively and empathize with all parties involved reflects the Philippians mindset of seeking understanding and resolution.

3. Forgiveness as a Path to Healing: Philippians Reconciliation

Embrace forgiveness as a powerful path to healing in conflicts. Explore how the Philippians mindset of forgetting the past and pressing forward aligns with the transformative impact of forgiveness in resolving conflicts.

Example: The Truth and Reconciliation Commission in South Africa

Examine the Truth and Reconciliation Commission in South Africa as a model for forgiveness and healing. The commission's commitment to acknowledging past wrongs and facilitating forgiveness aligns with the Philippians principle of pressing on toward reconciliation.

4. Seeking Common Ground: Philippians Unity

Strive for unity by seeking common ground in conflicts. Explore how finding shared goals and values aligns with the Philippians mindset of pressing forward toward a common purpose, fostering resolution and understanding.

Example: The Camp David Accords

Examine the Camp David Accords as a historical example of seeking common ground. The agreement between Egypt and Israel demonstrates the power of finding shared objectives, reflecting the Philippians principle of unity in conflict resolution.

5. Constructive Communication: Philippians Clarity

Communicate with clarity and constructive intent in conflict resolution. Explore how expressing thoughts and feelings with the aim of mutual understanding aligns with the Philippians principle of intentional communication.

Example: The Marshall Plan's Diplomatic Communication

Study the Marshall Plan's diplomatic communication during post-World War II reconstruction. The clarity of communication and mutual understanding among participating nations reflects the Philippians mindset of intentional and constructive dialogue.

Applying Philippians Principles to Conflict Resolution Mastery

Apply the principles derived from Philippians to master the art of conflict resolution, offering actionable insights for fostering understanding, reconciliation, and lasting peace.

1. Humility as a Conflict Resolution Skill

Cultivate humility as a skill in conflict resolution. Learn practical strategies for approaching conflicts with humility, fostering an atmosphere of openness and understanding.

2. Empathy in Action

Put empathy into action in conflict resolution. Explore exercises and techniques for actively listening and empathizing, building bridges of understanding in challenging situations.

3. The Art of Forgiveness

Master the art of forgiveness in conflict resolution. Discover transformative practices for letting go of resentment and embracing forgiveness, aligning with the Philippians principle of pressing forward in reconciliation.

Your Conflict Resolution Mastery Toolkit: Practical Strategies for Daily Application

As you conclude this chapter, discover practical tools and exercises to integrate the Philippians approach to conflict resolution into your daily life. These tools will serve as your allies in cultivating continuous growth, purposeful focus, and unwavering commitment as you navigate conflicts with grace and seek harmonious resolutions.

Chapter Twenty-Three: Philippians and Emotional Intelligence

Embark on an illuminating exploration into the realm of emotional intelligence, guided by the timeless wisdom of Philippians 3:12-14. In this chapter, unravel the profound connection between emotional intelligence and the Philippians mindset of continuous growth, purposeful focus, and unwavering commitment, paving the way for personal and professional excellence.

Philippians 3:12-14: Elevating Emotional Intelligence

"I don't mean to say that I have already achieved these things or that I have already reached perfection. But I press on to possess that perfection for which Christ Jesus first possessed me. No, dear brothers and sisters, I have not achieved it, but I focus on this one thing: Forgetting the past and looking forward to what lies ahead, I press on to reach the end of the race and receive the heavenly prize for which God, through Christ Jesus, is calling us." - Philippians 3:12-14 (NLT)

Let these verses serve as a guide to elevate emotional intelligence, where continuous growth, purposeful focus, and unwavering commitment converge to cultivate self-awareness, empathy, and effective interpersonal relationships.

1. Self-Awareness: Philippians Reflection

Cultivate self-awareness through the lens of Philippians reflection. Explore how the practice of introspection and acknowledging personal strengths and weaknesses aligns with the Philippians mindset of continuous self-improvement.

Example: Socrates' Know Thyself

Delve into the ancient Greek philosophy of "Know Thyself" attributed to Socrates. The pursuit of self-awareness through reflection mirrors the Philippians principle of pressing on toward personal perfection.

2. Self-Regulation: Philippians Discipline

Practice self-regulation guided by Philippians discipline. Explore how cultivating emotional control, particularly in challenging situations, aligns with the Philippians mindset of purposeful focus and unwavering commitment.

Example: Nelson Mandela's Imprisonment

Reflect on Nelson Mandela's imprisonment and the discipline he maintained. Mandela's ability to regulate his emotions during challenging times aligns with the Philippians principle of pressing on despite adversities.

3. Motivation and Purpose: Philippians Drive

Fuel motivation and purpose through the Philippians drive for excellence. Explore how aligning personal and professional goals with a higher purpose resonates with the Philippians mindset of pressing on toward a heavenly calling.

Example: Marie Curie's Scientific Passion

Examine Marie Curie's unwavering passion for scientific discovery. Curie's motivation aligns with the Philippians principle of pressing on toward perfection, leaving a legacy of groundbreaking contributions.

4. Empathy and Understanding: Philippians Compassion

Cultivate empathy and understanding with a Philippians spirit of compassion. Explore how considering others as more significant than oneself fosters meaningful connections and aligns with the Philippians mindset of empathy.

Example: Princess Diana's Humanitarian Efforts

Reflect on Princess Diana's humanitarian efforts. Her empathetic approach to social issues aligns with the Philippians principle of considering others, leaving a legacy of compassion and understanding.

5. Interpersonal Relationships: Philippians Unity

Nurture interpersonal relationships with the Philippians spirit of unity. Explore how fostering a sense of unity, mutual respect, and collaboration aligns with the Philippians mindset of considering the needs of others.

Example: Martin Luther King Jr.'s Civil Rights Movement

Examine Martin Luther King Jr.'s leadership in the Civil Rights Movement. His ability to build unity and relationships aligns with the Philippians principle of considering others, leaving a legacy of positive change.

Applying Philippians Principles to Emotional Intelligence Mastery

Apply the principles derived from Philippians to master the art of emotional intelligence, offering actionable insights for cultivating self-awareness, self-regulation, motivation, empathy, and fostering harmonious relationships.

1. Daily Practices for Self-Awareness

Incorporate daily practices for self-awareness into your routine. Explore exercises and techniques that align with the Philippians principle of continuous self-reflection for personal growth.

2. Strategies for Emotional Regulation

Develop strategies for emotional regulation inspired by Philippians discipline. Learn practical techniques for maintaining emotional control in various situations, fostering resilience and purposeful focus.

3. Aligning Goals with Purpose

Align personal and professional goals with a higher purpose. Explore the process of connecting your aspirations with a greater calling, in line with the Philippians principle of pressing on toward a heavenly prize.

Your Emotional Intelligence Mastery Toolkit: Practical Strategies for Daily Application

As you conclude this chapter, discover practical tools and exercises to integrate the Philippians approach to emotional intelligence mastery into your daily life. These tools will serve as your allies in cultivating continuous growth, purposeful focus, and unwavering commitment as you elevate your emotional intelligence and leave a lasting impact on your personal and professional relationships.

Chapter Twenty-Four: Soccer - Strategies for Team Focus

Embark on an exhilarating exploration of team focus in the context of soccer, guided by the timeless wisdom of Philippians 3:12-14. In this chapter, unravel the dynamic connection between the principles of continuous growth, purposeful focus, and unwavering commitment from Philippians, and the strategies that elevate soccer teams to excellence, fostering a spirit of unity and achievement.

Philippians 3:12-14: Elevating Team Focus

"I don't mean to say that I have already achieved these things or that I have already reached perfection. But I press on to possess that perfection for which Christ Jesus first possessed me. No, dear brothers and sisters, I have not achieved it, but I focus on this one thing: Forgetting the past and looking forward to what lies ahead, I press on to reach the end of the race and receive the heavenly prize for which God, through Christ Jesus, is calling us." - Philippians 3:12-14 (NLT)

Let these verses be the guiding force behind strategies for team focus in soccer, where continuous growth, purposeful focus, and unwavering commitment converge to create a winning culture.

1. Continuous Improvement in Training: Philippians Dedication

Instill a sense of continuous improvement in team training inspired by Philippians dedication. Explore how the commitment to refining skills and strategies aligns with the Philippians mindset of pressing on toward perfection.

Example: FC Barcelona's Tiki-Taka Style

Delve into FC Barcelona's Tiki-Taka style of play. The team's dedication to intricate passing and continuous training aligns with the Philippians principle of pressing on toward perfection, resulting in a distinctive and successful playing style.

2. Maintaining Focus During Matches: Philippians Resilience

Cultivate resilience and focus during matches, drawing inspiration from Philippians resilience. Explore how the ability to bounce back from setbacks aligns with the Philippians mindset of pressing on despite challenges.

Example: Germany's 2014 World Cup Comeback

Reflect on Germany's comeback in the 2014 World Cup against Brazil. The team's resilience and ability to maintain focus in the face of adversity align with the Philippians principle of pressing on toward the goal.

3. Team Unity and Communication: Philippians Collaboration

Foster team unity and communication grounded in Philippians collaboration. Explore how effective communication and a sense of unity align with the Philippians mindset of considering others as more significant than oneself.

Example: Spain's 2010 World Cup Winning Team

Examine Spain's 2010 World Cup-winning team. The team's collaboration and unity on and off the field align with the Philippians principle of considering others, resulting in a harmonious and successful squad.

4. Goal setting and Vision: Philippians Purpose

Set goals and establish a clear vision inspired by Philippians purpose. Explore how defining a common objective and vision aligns with the Philippians mindset of pressing on toward a heavenly prize.

Example: Leicester City's Premier League Title

Study Leicester City's historic Premier League title win in 2015-2016. The team's clear vision and commitment to their goals align with the Philippians principle of pressing on toward a higher achievement.

5. Celebrating Success and Learning from Failure: Philippians Gratitude

Cultivate a culture of gratitude in celebrating success and learning from failure, drawing from Philippians gratitude. Explore how acknowledging achievements and setbacks aligns with the Philippians mindset of pressing on with a thankful heart.

Example: Real Madrid's Champions League Dominance

Explore Real Madrid's success in the UEFA Champions League. The team's ability to celebrate victories and learn from defeats aligns with the Philippians principle of pressing on with gratitude.

Applying Philippians Principles to Soccer Team Focus Mastery

Apply the principles derived from Philippians to master the art of team focus in soccer, offering actionable insights for fostering continuous improvement, resilience, unity, goal-setting, and a culture of gratitude.

1. Team Building Activities for Unity

Incorporate team-building activities to foster unity. Explore exercises that align with the Philippians principle of considering others as more significant than oneself, creating a cohesive and collaborative team environment.

2. Resilience Training for Adversity

Implement resilience training to navigate adversity. Learn practical strategies inspired by Philippians resilience, preparing the team to overcome challenges and maintain focus during critical moments.

3. Vision Setting for Goal Achievement

Establish vision-setting sessions for goal achievement. Explore techniques that align with the Philippians principle of pressing on toward a higher achievement, ensuring the team's objectives are clear and purposeful.

Your Soccer Team Focus Mastery Toolkit: Practical Strategies for Daily Application

As you conclude this chapter, discover practical tools and exercises to integrate the Philippians approach to soccer team focus mastery into your training routines. These tools will serve as your allies in cultivating continuous growth, purposeful focus, and unwavering commitment, propelling your soccer team toward excellence, and creating a legacy of success on the field.

Chapter Twenty-Five: NBA Basketball - Individual Excellence through Focus

Embark on an inspiring exploration of individual excellence in NBA Basketball, guided by the profound wisdom of Philippians 3:12-14. In this chapter, discover the intricate connection between continuous growth, purposeful focus, and unwavering commitment from Philippians, and the strategies that propel NBA players to reach new heights of individual brilliance, fostering a legacy of greatness.

Philippians 3:12-14: Elevating Individual Excellence

"I don't mean to say that I have already achieved these things or that I have already reached perfection. But I press on to possess that perfection for which Christ Jesus first possessed me. No, dear brothers and sisters, I have not achieved it, but I focus on this one thing: Forgetting the past and looking forward to what lies ahead, I press on to reach the end of the race and receive the heavenly prize for which God, through Christ Jesus, is calling us." - Philippians 3:12-14 (NLT)

Let these verses serve as the cornerstone for strategies that elevate individual excellence in NBA Basketball, where continuous growth, purposeful focus, and unwavering commitment converge to create a legacy of greatness.

1. Continuous Skill Development: Philippians Mastery

Pursue continuous skill development inspired by Philippians mastery. Explore how the commitment to refining basketball skills aligns with the Philippians mindset of pressing on toward perfection.

Example: Kobe Bryant's Mamba Mentality

Delve into Kobe Bryant's Mamba Mentality. Bryant's relentless pursuit of skill mastery and continuous improvement aligns with the Philippians principle of pressing on toward perfection, leaving an indelible mark on the game.

2. Mental Toughness and Focus: Philippians Resilience

Cultivate mental toughness and focus during games, drawing inspiration from Philippians resilience. Explore how the ability to maintain concentration and bounce back from setbacks aligns with the Philippians mindset of pressing on despite challenges.

Example: Michael Jordan's Clutch Performances

Reflect on Michael Jordan's clutch performances. Jordan's mental toughness and ability to focus in critical moments align with the Philippians principle of pressing on toward the goal, solidifying his status as one of the greatest players in NBA history.

3. Goal Setting and Career Vision: Philippians Purpose

Set individual goals and establish a clear vision inspired by Philippians purpose. Explore how defining personal objectives and aligning them with a higher purpose aligns with the Philippians mindset of pressing on toward a heavenly prize.

Example: LeBron James' Longevity and Consistency

Study LeBron James' career longevity and consistent success. James' ability to set and achieve long-term goals aligns with the Philippians principle of pressing on toward a higher achievement, creating a lasting legacy.

4. Embracing Challenges and Growth: Philippians Acceptance

Embrace challenges and foster personal growth, drawing from Philippians acceptance. Explore how acknowledging weaknesses and using challenges as opportunities aligns with the Philippians mindset of pressing on toward perfection.

Example: Stephen Curry's Revolutionary Shooting Style

Examine Stephen Curry's revolutionary shooting style. Curry's acceptance of unconventional methods and continuous growth aligns with the Philippians principle of pressing on toward perfection, transforming the game of basketball.

5. Maintaining Humility and Team Collaboration: Philippians Unity

Nurture humility and collaborate effectively with teammates, grounded in Philippians unity. Explore how maintaining humility and considering teammates as more significant than oneself aligns with the Philippians mindset of unity.

Example: Tim Duncan's Team-First Mentality

Reflect on Tim Duncan's team-first mentality. Duncan's humility and collaborative approach align with the Philippians principle of considering others, contributing to his success and impact on the NBA.

Applying Philippians Principles to NBA Basketball Mastery

Apply the principles derived from Philippians to master the art of individual excellence in NBA Basketball, offering actionable insights for fostering continuous skill development, mental toughness, goal setting, embracing challenges, and maintaining humility.

1. Personalized Skill Development Plan

Craft a personalized skill development plan. Explore exercises and drills that align with the Philippians principle of continuous improvement, enhancing your basketball skills and contributing to individual excellence.

2. Mental Toughness Training Routine

Establish a mental toughness training routine. Learn practical strategies inspired by Philippians resilience to maintain focus during games, handle pressure, and bounce back from setbacks.

3. Goal-Setting Framework for Career Success

Develop a goal-setting framework for career success. Explore techniques that align with the Philippians principle of pressing on toward a higher achievement, ensuring personal objectives contribute to a lasting legacy.

Your NBA Basketball Mastery Toolkit: Practical Strategies for Daily Application

As you conclude this chapter, discover practical tools and exercises to integrate the Philippians approach to NBA Basketball mastery into your training regimen. These tools will serve as your allies in cultivating continuous growth, purposeful focus, and unwavering commitment, propelling you toward individual excellence, and leaving a lasting impact on the court.

Chapter Twenty-Six: NFL Football - Team Dynamics and Moving Forward

Embark on an invigorating exploration of team dynamics in NFL Football, guided by the profound wisdom of Philippians 3:12-14. In this chapter, unravel the intricate connection between continuous growth, purposeful focus, and unwavering commitment from Philippians, and the strategies that propel NFL teams to forge a path of triumph, emphasizing teamwork and a relentless drive to move forward.

Philippians 3:12-14: Elevating Team Dynamics

"I don't mean to say that I have already achieved these things or that I have already reached perfection. But I press on to possess that perfection for which Christ Jesus first possessed me. No, dear brothers and sisters, I have not achieved it, but I focus on this one thing: Forgetting the past and looking forward to what lies ahead, I press on to reach the end of the race and receive the heavenly prize for which God, through Christ Jesus, is calling us." - Philippians 3:12-14 (NLT)

Let these verses illuminate the strategies that elevate team dynamics in NFL Football, where continuous growth, purposeful focus, and unwavering commitment converge to create a legacy of triumph and moving forward.

1. Collective Goal Pursuit: Philippians Unity

Pursue collective goal pursuit inspired by Philippians unity. Explore how the commitment to a shared objective and team success aligns with the Philippians mindset of pressing on toward a higher calling.

Example: New England Patriots' Dynasty Era

Delve into the New England Patriots' dynasty era. The team's commitment to collective success, epitomized by multiple Super Bowl victories, aligns with the Philippians principle of pressing on toward a heavenly prize.

2. Adaptive Strategies and Resilience: Philippians Flexibility

Cultivate adaptive strategies and resilience during games, drawing inspiration from Philippians flexibility. Explore how the ability to adjust to challenges and bounce back from setbacks aligns with the Philippians mindset of pressing on despite obstacles.

Example: Kansas City Chiefs' Dynamic Offense

Reflect on the Kansas City Chiefs' dynamic offense. The team's adaptive strategies and resilience, especially in high-pressure situations, align with the Philippians principle of pressing on toward the goal.

3. Collective Accountability and Brotherhood: Philippians Consideration

Foster collective accountability and brotherhood grounded in Philippians consideration. Explore how holding each other accountable and considering teammates as more significant than oneself aligns with the Philippians mindset of unity.

Example: Baltimore Ravens' Defensive Dominance

Examine the Baltimore Ravens' defensive dominance. The team's collective accountability and brotherhood, showcased in their formidable defense, align with the Philippians principle of considering others, contributing to their success.

4. Learning from Setbacks and Continuous Improvement: Philippians Growth

Embrace setbacks as opportunities for learning and continuous improvement, drawing from Philippians growth. Explore how acknowledging weaknesses and using challenges to evolve aligns with the Philippians mindset of pressing on toward perfection.

Example: Green Bay Packers' Resilience

Study the Green Bay Packers' resilience in the face of setbacks. The team's ability to learn from challenges and continuously improve aligns with the Philippians principle of pressing on toward perfection.

5. Legacy Building and Community Impact: Philippians Impact

Nurture a culture of legacy building and community impact, grounded in Philippians impact. Explore how leaving a lasting legacy on and off the field aligns with the Philippians mindset of pressing on toward a heavenly prize.

Example: Pittsburgh Steelers' Imprint on Community

Reflect on the Pittsburgh Steelers' impact on the community. The team's commitment to legacy building and community engagement aligns with the Philippians principle of pressing on toward a higher achievement.

Applying Philippians Principles to NFL Football Mastery

Apply the principles derived from Philippians to master the dynamics of NFL Football, offering actionable insights for pursuing collective goals, fostering resilience, building brotherhood, embracing growth, and leaving a lasting impact.

1. Team-Building Exercises for Unity

Incorporate team-building exercises to foster unity. Explore activities that align with the Philippians principle of considering others as more significant than oneself, creating a cohesive and collaborative team environment.

2. Resilience Training for Adversity

Implement resilience training to navigate adversity. Learn practical strategies inspired by Philippians flexibility, preparing the team to adapt to challenges and bounce back from setbacks.

3. Legacy-Building Initiatives for Community Impact

Establish legacy-building initiatives for community impact. Explore approaches that align with the Philippians principle of pressing on toward a heavenly prize, ensuring the team's influence extends beyond the field.

Your NFL Football Mastery Toolkit: Practical Strategies for Daily Application

As you conclude this chapter, discover practical tools and exercises to integrate the Philippians approach to NFL Football mastery into your team's routines. These tools will serve as your allies in cultivating continuous growth, purposeful focus, and unwavering commitment, propelling your NFL team toward triumph and leaving an enduring legacy in the realm of football.

Chapter Twenty-Seven: Family Harmony with Philippians Values

Embark on a heartwarming exploration of family harmony, guided by the profound wisdom of Philippians 3:12-14. In this chapter, uncover the delicate interplay between continuous growth, purposeful focus, and unwavering commitment from Philippians, and the strategies that foster an environment of love, unity, and moving forward within the family.

Philippians 3:12-14: Elevating Family Harmony

"I don't mean to say that I have already achieved these things or that I have already reached perfection. But I press on to possess that perfection for which Christ Jesus first possessed me. No, dear brothers and sisters, I have not achieved it, but I focus on this one thing: Forgetting the past and looking forward to what lies ahead, I press on to reach the end of the race and receive the heavenly prize for which God, through Christ Jesus, is calling us." - Philippians 3:12-14 (NLT)

Let these verses illuminate the strategies that elevate family harmony, where continuous growth, purposeful focus, and unwavering commitment converge to create a haven of love, understanding, and moving forward.

1. Shared Family Goals: Philippians Unity

Cultivate shared family goals inspired by Philippians unity. Explore how setting common objectives and working together as a family align with the Philippians mindset of pressing on toward a higher calling.

Example: The Johnson Family Adventure Journal

Embark on the Johnson family's adventure journal. By setting goals like exploring new places together, they exemplify the Philippians principle of pressing on toward a heavenly prize, creating lasting memories and reinforcing family bonds.

2. Effective Communication and Understanding: Philippians Consideration

Foster effective communication and understanding grounded in Philippians consideration. Explore how listening and considering each family member's perspective align with the Philippians mindset of unity.

Example: The Patel Family Weekly Check-ins

Experience the Patel family's weekly check-ins. By creating a space for open communication, they embody the Philippians principle of considering others as more significant than oneself, building a foundation of trust and understanding.

3. Resilience in Family Challenges: Philippians Acceptance

Embrace resilience in the face of family challenges, drawing inspiration from Philippians acceptance. Explore how acknowledging imperfections and embracing challenges align with the Philippians mindset of pressing on toward perfection.

Example: The Rodriguez Family's Journey Through Loss

Witness the Rodriguez family's journey through loss. By leaning on each other and finding strength in adversity, they embody the Philippians principle of pressing on toward perfection, fostering resilience and unity.

4. Cultivating a Culture of Gratitude: Philippians Gratitude

Nurture a culture of gratitude within the family, grounded in Philippians gratitude. Explore how expressing thankfulness for each other aligns with the Philippians mindset of pressing on with a thankful heart.

Example: The Anderson Family Gratitude Jar

Discover the Anderson family's gratitude jar. By regularly acknowledging and appreciating each other's contributions, they embody the Philippians principle of pressing on with gratitude, creating a positive and uplifting atmosphere.

5. Teaching and Modeling Philippians Values: Philippians Impact

Instill Philippians values in family life and relationships. Explore how teaching and modeling continuous growth, purposeful focus, and unwavering commitment align with the Philippians mindset of pressing on toward a heavenly prize.

Example: The Thompson Family's Philippians Night

Join the Thompson family's Philippians night. By incorporating Bible study and discussions centered around Philippians values, they exemplify the Philippians principle of pressing on toward a higher achievement, nurturing spiritual growth within the family.

Applying Philippians Principles to Family Harmony Mastery

Apply the principles derived from Philippians to master family harmony, offering actionable insights for setting shared goals, fostering effective communication, embracing resilience, cultivating gratitude, and teaching Philippians values.

1. Family Vision Board for Shared Goals

Create a family vision board for shared goals. Explore activities and discussions that align with the Philippians principle of pressing on toward a higher calling, ensuring family members actively contribute to the family's aspirations.

2. Communication Techniques for Understanding

Implement communication techniques for better understanding. Learn practical strategies inspired by Philippians consideration, promoting active listening and creating a supportive environment within the family.

3. Resilience-Building Exercises for Challenges

Incorporate resilience-building exercises for family challenges. Explore approaches that align with the Philippians principle of pressing on toward perfection, fostering a resilient mindset within the family.

Your Family Harmony Mastery Toolkit: Practical Strategies for Daily Application

As you conclude this chapter, discover practical tools and exercises to integrate the Philippians approach to family harmony mastery into your daily family life. These tools will serve as your allies in cultivating continuous growth, purposeful focus, and unwavering commitment, creating a haven of love, unity, and moving forward within your family.

Chapter Twenty-Eight: Global Citizenship - Impactful Actions with Focus

Embark on a transformative journey towards global citizenship, guided by the profound wisdom of Philippians 3:12-14. In this chapter, explore the intersection of continuous growth, purposeful focus, and unwavering commitment from Philippians, unveiling the strategies that empower individuals to make a meaningful impact on a global scale through focused actions.

Philippians 3:12-14: Elevating Global *Citizenship*

"I don't mean to say that I have already achieved these things or that I have already reached perfection. But I press on to possess that perfection for which Christ Jesus first possessed me. No, dear brothers and sisters, I have not achieved it, but I focus on this one thing: Forgetting the past and looking forward to what lies ahead, I press on to reach the end of the race and receive the heavenly prize for which God, through Christ Jesus, is calling us." - Philippians 3:12-14 (NLT)

Let these verses inspire the strategies that elevate global citizenship, where continuous growth, purposeful focus, and unwavering commitment converge to create a positive impact on a worldwide scale.

1. Philanthropy with Purpose: Philippians Generosity

Engage in philanthropy with purpose inspired by Philippians generosity. Explore how contributing to causes that align with global well-being aligns with the Philippians mindset of pressing on toward a higher calling.

Example: The Smith Foundation's Clean Water Initiatives

Witness the impact of the Smith Foundation's clean water initiatives. By investing in projects that provide clean water in impoverished regions, they exemplify the Philippians principle of pressing on toward a heavenly prize, making a significant contribution to global health.

2. Advocacy for Social Justice: Philippians Righteousness

Champion advocacy for social justice grounded in Philippians righteousness. Explore how raising awareness and standing up for the oppressed aligns with the Philippians mindset of pressing on despite societal challenges.

Example: Maria's Global Campaign Against Human Trafficking

Follow Maria's global campaign against human trafficking. By dedicating her efforts to raise awareness and combat this injustice, she embodies the Philippians principle of pressing on toward a higher achievement, striving for righteousness on a global scale.

3. Sustainable Living and Environmental Stewardship: Philippians Care

Embrace sustainable living and environmental stewardship inspired by Philippians care. Explore how mindful consumption and conservation efforts align with the Philippians mindset of pressing on toward perfection for the greater good.

Example: The Green Earth Initiative

Explore the impact of the Green Earth Initiative. By promoting sustainable practices and environmental education globally, they embody the Philippians principle of pressing on toward perfection, caring for the Earth as responsible global citizens.

4. Cultural Understanding and Unity: Philippians Harmony

Cultivate cultural understanding and unity grounded in Philippians harmony. Explore how embracing diversity and fostering international collaborations align with the Philippians mindset of pressing on toward a common goal.

Example: Global Friendship Exchange Program

Engage in the Global Friendship Exchange Program. By fostering cultural exchanges and promoting international understanding, they exemplify the Philippians principle of considering others as more significant than oneself, building bridges across borders.

5. Educational Initiatives for Global Access: Philippians Knowledge

Support educational initiatives for global access inspired by Philippians knowledge. Explore how promoting education and facilitating learning opportunities align with the Philippians mindset of pressing on toward a heavenly prize for the betterment of humanity.

Example: The Open Minds Project

Witness the impact of the Open Minds Project. By providing educational resources and opportunities globally, they embody the Philippians principle of pressing on toward a higher achievement, empowering individuals worldwide through knowledge.

Applying Philippians Principles to Global Citizenship Mastery

Apply the principles derived from Philippians to master global citizenship, offering actionable insights for philanthropy, advocacy, sustainable living, cultural understanding, and educational initiatives.

1. Impactful Giving Strategies

Develop impactful giving strategies. Explore ways to align your philanthropic efforts with causes that resonate with the Philippians principle of pressing on toward a higher calling, maximizing your positive impact on a global scale.

2. Advocacy Campaign Planning

Create effective advocacy campaign plans. Learn practical strategies inspired by Philippians righteousness to raise awareness and stand up for social justice issues, contributing to positive global change.

3. Sustainable Lifestyle Action Plan

Adopt a sustainable lifestyle action plan. Explore practices that align with the Philippians principle of pressing on toward perfection, contributing to environmental stewardship and global well-being.

Your Global Citizenship Mastery Toolkit: Practical Strategies for Daily Application

As you conclude this chapter, discover practical tools and exercises to integrate the Philippians approach to global citizenship mastery into your daily life. These tools will serve as your allies in cultivating continuous growth, purposeful focus, and unwavering commitment, making a lasting impact on a global scale through focused and intentional actions.

Chapter Twenty-Nine: Environmental Stewardship and Philippians Principles

Embark on a transformative exploration of environmental stewardship, guided by the profound wisdom of Philippians 3:12-14. In this chapter, discover the harmonious connection between continuous growth, purposeful focus, and unwavering commitment from Philippians, unveiling the strategies that empower individuals to become stewards of the Earth through intentional actions and a mindset of pressing on toward a higher calling.

Philippians 3:12-14: Elevating Environmental Stewardship

"I don't mean to say that I have already achieved these things or that I have already reached perfection. But I press on to possess that perfection for which Christ Jesus first possessed me. No, dear brothers and sisters, I have not achieved it, but I focus on this one thing: Forgetting the past and looking forward to what lies ahead, I press on to reach the end of the race and receive the heavenly prize for which God, through Christ Jesus, is calling us." - Philippians 3:12-14 (NLT)

Let these verses inspire the strategies that elevate environmental stewardship, where continuous growth, purposeful focus, and unwavering commitment converge to create a positive impact on the Earth.

1. Mindful Consumption and Simplified Living: Philippians Contentment

Embrace mindful consumption and simplified living inspired by Philippians contentment. Explore how reducing materialism and adopting a minimalist lifestyle align with the Philippians mindset of pressing on toward perfection for the greater good.

Example: The Johnson Family's Minimalist Journey

Witness the Johnson family's minimalist journey. By embracing a simpler lifestyle and making mindful choices in consumption, they embody the Philippians principle of pressing on toward perfection, contributing to a reduction in environmental impact.

2. Conservation and Restoration Initiatives: Philippians Renewal

Engage in conservation and restoration initiatives grounded in Philippians renewal. Explore how participating in efforts to preserve and restore ecosystems align with the Philippians mindset of pressing on despite challenges for the well-being of the Earth.

Example: The Green Earth Alliance's Reforestation Project

Experience the impact of the Green Earth Alliance's reforestation project. By actively participating in initiatives to renew and restore forests, they exemplify the Philippians principle of pressing on toward a heavenly prize, contributing to the Earth's rejuvenation.

3. Sustainable Practices in Daily Life: Philippians Holiness

Incorporate sustainable practices into daily life inspired by Philippians holiness. Explore how adopting eco-friendly habits and promoting sustainable choices align with the Philippians mindset of pressing on toward a higher calling for the Earth's sanctity.

Example: Sarah's Sustainable Living Blog

Explore Sarah's sustainable living blog. By sharing practical tips and advocating for sustainable choices, she embodies the Philippians principle of pressing on toward a higher achievement, inspiring others to adopt holiness in their daily interactions with the environment.

4. Environmental Education and Advocacy: Philippians Knowledge

Champion environmental education and advocacy grounded in Philippians knowledge. Explore how spreading awareness and advocating for sustainable policies align with the Philippians mindset of pressing on toward a heavenly prize for the Earth's betterment.

Example: The Eco Warriors Club in Schools

Engage with the Eco Warriors Club in schools. By promoting environmental education and advocating for sustainable practices, they exemplify the Philippians principle of pressing on toward perfection, empowering future generations with knowledge.

5. Corporate Responsibility and Green Initiatives: Philippians Integrity

Support corporate responsibility and green initiatives inspired by Philippians integrity. Explore how holding businesses accountable for sustainable practices aligns with the Philippians mindset of pressing on despite obstacles for the Earth's integrity.

Example: The Sustainable Business Certification Program

Learn about the Sustainable Business Certification Program. By encouraging businesses to adopt eco-friendly practices, they embody the Philippians principle of pressing on toward perfection, contributing to the Earth's integrity on a larger scale.

Applying Philippians Principles to Environmental Stewardship Mastery

Apply the principles derived from Philippians to master environmental stewardship, offering actionable insights for mindful consumption, conservation efforts, sustainable living, education, and corporate responsibility.

1. Eco-Friendly Lifestyle Transition Plan

Develop an eco-friendly lifestyle transition plan. Explore ways to align your daily choices with the Philippians principle of pressing on toward perfection, minimizing your environmental footprint and contributing to the Earth's well-being.

2. Community-Based Restoration Projects

Initiate community-based restoration projects. Learn practical strategies inspired by Philippians renewal to actively participate in restoring and preserving natural habitats, contributing to the Earth's rejuvenation.

3. Advocacy Campaigns for Sustainable Policies

Launch advocacy campaigns for sustainable policies. Explore ways to align your efforts with the Philippians principle of pressing on toward a higher calling, encouraging policies that promote environmental health and sustainability.

Your Environmental Stewardship Mastery Toolkit: Practical Strategies for Daily Application

As you conclude this chapter, discover practical tools and exercises to integrate the Philippians approach to environmental stewardship mastery into your daily life. These tools will serve as your allies in cultivating continuous growth, purposeful focus, and unwavering commitment, empowering you to become a dedicated steward of the Earth.

Chapter Thirty: Conclusion - Your Unstoppable Journey Begins

As we bring this transformative journey to a close, let the timeless wisdom of Philippians 3:12-14 resonate within you, becoming the driving force behind your unstoppable journey toward continuous growth, purposeful focus, and unwavering commitment.

Philippians 3:12-14: Your Guiding Light

"I don't mean to say that I have already achieved these things or that I have already reached perfection. But I press on to possess that perfection for which Christ Jesus first possessed me. No, dear brothers and sisters, I have not achieved it, but I focus on this one thing: Forgetting the past and looking forward to what lies ahead, I press on to reach the end of the race and receive the heavenly prize for which God, through Christ Jesus, is calling us." - Philippians 3:12-14 (NLT)

Let these verses be the guiding light that propels you forward, encouraging you to press on toward your own heavenly prize, a life filled with purpose, fulfillment, and unwavering commitment.

1. Reflecting on Your Journey

Take a moment to reflect on the journey you've undertaken through the pages of this book. Consider the insights gained, the challenges faced, and the triumphs celebrated. Your journey is unique, filled with potential waiting to be unleashed.

2. Embracing Continuous Growth

Acknowledge that the pursuit of perfection is not about reaching a destination but about the continuous journey of growth. Every step you take, every lesson learned, contributes to the person you are becoming.

3. Unleashing Purposeful Focus

Recognize the power of purposeful focus. By embracing a mindset that looks forward and forgets the past, you pave the way for intentional living. Your goals, dreams, and aspirations become clearer, and your actions align with the person you strive to be.

4. Cultivating Unwavering Commitment

Embrace unwavering commitment to your goals, values, and the principles that guide your journey. Just as Paul pressed on toward the heavenly prize, you too can press on with determination, resilience, and a steadfast spirit.

5. Your Unstoppable Journey Begins

As you conclude this book, understand that your unstoppable journey begins now. Armed with the wisdom of Philippians, you are equipped to face challenges, embrace growth, and live a life filled with purpose. Your journey is a testament to the transformative power of continuous learning and unwavering commitment.

Applying Philippians Principles Beyond the Pages

Apply the principles you've discovered beyond the pages of this book. Let Philippians be the foundation upon which you build a life of significance. Use the lessons learned to navigate the complexities of the modern world and let the transformative power of Philippians guide your decisions, actions, and interactions.

Your Personal Commitment to Unstoppable Living

Craft a personal commitment to living an unstoppable life. Set specific goals, align them with the principles of Philippians, and let this commitment serve as a beacon, guiding you through the challenges and triumphs that lie ahead.

Continuing the Journey

This book is not the end but a catalyst for a lifelong journey. The principles of Philippians will continue to inspire and guide you. Seek out new opportunities for growth, discover fresh perspectives, and press on toward the ever-evolving vision of your heavenly prize.

A World Transformed

Imagine a world where individuals, inspired by the principles of Philippians, press on toward a collective heavenly prize of unity, purpose, and unwavering commitment. As you apply these principles in your life, you contribute to the transformation of the world around you.

Thank You for Being a Part of This Journey

Finally, I extend my heartfelt gratitude for being a part of this journey. Your commitment to continuous learning, growth, and living with purpose has the potential to create ripples of positive change that extend far beyond the confines of these pages.

May your unstoppable journey be filled with purpose, joy, and the fulfillment that comes from pressing on toward the heavenly prize that awaits you. Your adventure has just begun. Press on, embrace the journey, and let the principles of Philippians be your guiding light.

Inviting Future Explorations

As you close this chapter, consider this not as an end but as an invitation to future explorations. The wisdom of Philippians is vast and timeless, offering endless opportunities for deeper understanding and application.

1. Engaging in Community Discussions

Join or initiate community discussions centered around the principles of Philippians. Share your insights, challenges, and triumphs with others who have embarked on a similar journey. The collective wisdom of a community can fuels your unstoppable pursuit of growth and purpose.

2. Integrating Philippians into Daily Practices

Make Philippians a part of your daily practices. Incorporate moments of reflection, prayer, or mindfulness inspired by the verses. Let the teachings permeate your decision-making, interactions, and responses to life's challenges.

3. Continuing Education and Learning

Continue your education and learning journey. Explore additional resources, whether books, articles, or lectures, that delve into the teachings of Philippians. The more you immerse yourself in this wisdom, the more profound its impact on your life.

4. Inspiring Others with Your Journey

Share your journey with others. Your story has the potential to inspire and motivate those around you. Whether through writing, speaking, or leading by example, your commitment to an unstoppable life can create a positive ripple effect in your community.

5. Setting New Goals and Aspirations

Set new goals and aspirations for the future. Philippians provide a solid foundation for personal and spiritual growth. Use this knowledge to envision a future that aligns with your values, passions, and the heavenly prize you are pressing on toward.

A Lasting Impact

Your engagement with the teachings of Philippians has the power to create a lasting impact, not only in your life but in the lives of those you touch. Imagine a world where individuals, inspired by the unstoppable journey of continuous growth, purposeful focus, and unwavering commitment, contribute to a global transformation.

Thank You for Your Dedication

Thank you for dedicating yourself to this transformative journey. Your commitment to continuous learning, personal development, and the pursuit of an unstoppable life is commendable. May the principles of Philippians be a guiding light, illuminating your path toward a future filled with purpose, joy, and unwavering commitment.

Your Unstoppable Journey Awaits

As you turn the final page, remember that your unstoppable journey is not bound by the confines of a book. It is a dynamic, ever-unfolding adventure that you shape with each step, each decision, and each interaction. With the principles of Philippians as your guide, your journey becomes a testament to the boundless potential within you.

Your unstoppable journey awaits. Press on, embrace the challenges, savor the victories, and let the transformative power of Philippians propel you toward a life of continuous growth, purposeful focus, and unwavering commitment. The adventure has just begun.

ABOUT THE AUTHOR

Derick Chibilu is an upcoming talented author and business professional based in Houston, Texas, where he resides with his beloved wife, Alice, and is known for his inspiring works. Derick holds an MBA from Capella University, a Bachelor of Business in Computer Information Systems from the University of Houston Downtown (UHD), and an Associate of Science in Business Administration from Delaware Tech.

As a born-again Christian, Derick's faith is integral to his life. He is an active member of the North Central Assemblies of God Church in Spring, Texas, where he finds strength and inspiration through fellowship with other believers. Derick strongly believes in God, family, and Christian family values, which are central themes in his writing.

Derick has written extensively on various subjects such as business, leadership, personal development, and Christian spirituality. His works are highly regarded for their clarity, insight, and practicality, making them valuable resources for readers from all backgrounds.

DERICK CHIBILU'S COMMITMENT to excellence is evident in everything he does. He is a dedicated professional who takes pride in his work and is constantly seeking new ways to improve himself and his craft. Whether he is writing a new book, delivering a speech, or leading a team, Derick brings passion and enthusiasm to every endeavor.

In summary, Derick Chibilu is an inspiring author and business professional who is making a positive impact on the world. His faith, his family, and his commitment to Christian values deeply influence his life and work. Through his writing, Derick has the power to inspire and uplift readers worldwide.

BOOKS BY MR. DERICK CHIBILU

> **Whimsical Wonders:** 50 Tales of Fictional Fun

> **Love As God Intended It:** Faith, Hope, and Love, But the greatest of these is love.

> **The Bible Storybook**: 50 Exciting Stories for Kids (Volume 1)

> **The Bible Storybook:** 46 Parables: Tales of God's Kingdom and Our Lives (Volume 2)

> **The Bible Storybook**: Exploring The Transformative Power of Faith and The Miraculous Acts of Christ (Volume 3)

> **Shadows of Deception** ~The Hidden Secrets~

> **The Basilica Heist**: Shadows Unveiled

> **Vanishing Chains:** As the intricate plot continues to unfold,

> **Whispers of the Silent Shadows"** Part one

> **Beyond the Veil of Celestial Whispers:** Part Two: The Saga Continues

> **The Prophet Elisha's Unseen Paths**

> **Divine Dwelling**: Unveiling the Mysteries of the Tabernacle

> **Divine Dialogue**: Unveiling the Power of A.C.T.S in the Lord's

> **Whispers of Dawn**: Journey of Healing and Rediscovery

Author Contact Information

For information and inquiries or to see other books by the author:

Email: *Thecblogger4@gmail.com*

Or

Visit Our Website at:

www.booksbyderickchibilu.com

Did you love *Unwavering Focus: Journey to Excellence through Philippians 3:12-14*? Then you should read *DIVINE DIALOGUE: UNVEILING THE POWER OF A.C.T.S. IN THE LORD'S PRAYER* by DERICK CHIBILU!

In "Divine Dialogue," we explore the profound essence of prayer as we unravel the intricacies of the Lord's Prayer through the lens of A.C.T.S. This meticulously crafted book comprises twenty enlightening chapters, each delving into a specific facet of A.C.T.S and its manifestation in the Lord's Prayer.

Chapter 1-5: Adoration

Understand the importance of Adoration, the first pillar of A.C.T.S, as we dissect the opening lines of the Lord's Prayer. Discover the transformative power of praising and exalting the Divine, setting the tone for an intimate connection with the Creator.

Chapter 6-10: Confession

Delve into the concept of Confession, the soul-baring acknowledgment of shortcomings. Explore the Lord's Prayer to understand how confession fosters spiritual growth and renewal, paving the way for a deeper relationship with the Almighty.

Chapter 11-15: Thanksgiving

Grasp the significance of gratitude in prayer by exploring the Thanksgiving aspect of A.C.T.S. Learn how the Lord's Prayer exemplifies the art of expressing gratitude, fostering a spirit of thankfulness that transcends the challenges of life.

Chapter 16-20: Supplications

Uncover the power of supplication, the final pillar of A.C.T.S, through a comprehensive analysis of the concluding sections of the Lord's Prayer. Explore the transformative impact of earnest requests and petitions, discovering the profound nature of seeking divine intervention.

In this insightful book, we go beyond mere words, providing a detailed exploration of the foundations of prayer and the intricacies of A.C.T.S. Each chapter offers a unique perspective, drawing connections between the Lord's Prayer and the timeless framework of Adoration, Confession, Thanksgiving, and Supplications.

With an emphasis on original content, "Divine Dialogue" serves as a prayer guide for newcomers and paves the way for seasoned believers seeking a deeper understanding of their spiritual practice. This book is a valuable resource for those who wish to embark on a transformative journey of continuous learning in their faith.

Read more at https://www.booksbyderickchibilu.com/.

About the Author

Derick Chibilu is an upcoming talented author and business professional based in Houston, Texas, where he resides with his beloved wife, Alice, and is known for his inspiring works. Derick holds an MBA from Capella University, a Bachelor of Business in Computer Information Systems from the University of Houston Downtown (UHD), and an Associate of Science in Business Administration from Delaware Tech.

As a born-again Christian, Derick's faith is an integral part of his life. He is an active member of the North Central Assemblies of God Church in Spring, Texas, where he finds strength and inspiration through fellowship with other believers. Derick strongly believes in God, family, and Christian family values, which are central themes in his writing.

Derick has written extensively on various subjects such as business, leadership, personal development, and Christian spirituality. His works are highly regarded for their clarity, insight, and practicality, making them valuable resources for readers from all backgrounds.

Derick Chibilu's commitment to excellence is evident in everything he does. He is a dedicated professional who takes pride in his work and is constantly seeking new ways to improve himself and his craft. Whether he is writing a new book, delivering a speech, or leading a team, Derick brings passion and enthusiasm to every endeavor.

In summary, Derick Chibilu is an inspiring author and business professional who is making a positive impact

Read more at https://www.booksbyderickchibilu.com/.